Writing Humor for More Than Laughs

By Phil Truman

To Phred—
my Phunny Phriend.
Best—
Phil

Published by AWOCBOOKS.COM Publishing, P.O. Box 2819, Denton, TX 76202, USA.

Manufactured in the United States of America

ISBN: 0-9797597-8-1

Visit the author's web site: http://www.PhilTruman.com

Dedicated to the memory of my indomitable and wise parents who, among many things, taught me the value of laughter.

Anna Irene and Henry Lavelle I love you and I miss you.

Acknowledgements

I want to thank my wife Darlene for her constant encouragement, patience, and belief in my ability as a writer, and for laughing at most of what I say and write, especially those times when I want her to.

Also, thanks to my partner and long-time great good friend "Lieutenant Dan" Case for his insistence that I write this book.

Special thanks to Peggy Fielding for her generous help in making this a better book to read, and to Charles "Chuck" Sasser for his advice, critique, and great sense of humor in allowing me to jab him in the ribs.

I also want to express appreciation to my Border Collie slash black Lab friend, Grover, who steadfastly served as my sounding board and part-time security guard through the entire writing of this book – except during thunderstorms, when he insisted on hiding under my desk – and is a funny, funny dog.

Write the vision;
make it plain upon tablets,
so he may run who reads it.
For still the vision awaits its time;
it hastens to the end – it will not lie.
If it seems slow, wait for it; it will surely come,
it will not delay.

Habakkuk 2:2-3

Contents

Foreword

When I speak to groups of people, I feel perfectly confident that somehow within that talk, I will be able to make my listeners laugh, usually several times, in fact.

Something happens to that ability when I sit down to write. I' ve tried to insert humor into my written work, whether fiction, or nonfiction. My so called humor mostly turns out to be so heavy-handed that the whole attempt falls flat. Long ago I resigned myself to the idea that eliminating any forays into comedy in my written work was probably best for me...and for my work.

But hey! I've just finished reading Phil Truman's *WRITING HUMOR FOR MORE THAN LAUGHS* and I've had an epiphany! Phil's tome has taught me something...and it was these truths. Humor, like all other types of writing. has distinct rules. Humor is divided into various types. All the types have names and describable aspects.

You mean, if I work at it, I too can learn to be funny on paper? Yep, that's what Phil said. If I am willing to follow the rules (which I didn't know existed) and if I practice, success will follow just as it did in other fields of authorship.

Hurrah!

I'm going to use *WRITING HUMOR FOR MORE THAN LAUGHS* as my new textbook and then we'll see. If

I can begin to make people smile at what I've written, then anyone else can do the same. What a concept.

Thanks Phil. I'm keeping your book. Watch for my reader's laughter down the road, friend. I think I can do this.

Peggy Fielding

July, 2003

Introduction

Many years ago, when I first broke into writing, I got some pretty sound advice from a person whom I've always regarded as one of my best mentors.

"Be sure to make the body round like a circle, then put a straight line down the right side from top to bottom with a little tail going off to the right," Marion Osborne told me. "Good job. That's called an A, now let's write a B."

Writing didn't come easy for me back in those days. For one thing, there was a war going on in Korea and one of my brothers was a Marine over there; for another, there were big chunks of wood in my writing paper. I'm not exactly sure if one had anything to do with the other, but in hindsight I think the Big Chief Tablet Company probably had to sell us American first graders a lesser quality of paper in their consumer products in order to support the war effort. Who knows?

The only thing I know for sure was that Douglas MacArthur wasn't making things any easier for us Trumans. While my brother and his buddies fought in the Punch Bowl and Cousin Harry was having his problems with The General, I was experiencing my own troubles with inferior writing materials. But with Miss Osborne's guidance, I persevered and made it through to the Z's by Christmas. Harry fired The General, and my brother made it home alive.

Eventually, the North Koreans and Chinese agreed to a truce with us and the South Koreans. And to show their good faith, they built a big fence all the way across the country at the 38th Parallel planting many thousand land mines between it and us. Then, in a gesture of friendship and peace, we did the same, or rather the South Koreans did. They scraped the land clean for several hundred yards between these two fences and staffed both sides with hundreds of men, guns, tanks, and artillery pieces pointed toward the other side. Ironically, some fifteen years later, I was conscripted and sent to help maintain that "peace" along those fences.

But that's neither here nor there. The point is, despite all the difficulties I faced, I continued to develop my writing skills to where I learned - I think it was about the eighth grade - you could actually put two or more words together to form, what's called in the trade, sentences. And further, you could put several sentences together to create paragraphs, then pages, chapters, and books. Don't worry about these technical terms; we'll get into these later, and it will all start to make sense.

So what I want to do in the pages and chapters that follow, is impart to you all the vast knowledge I've learned since that golden day in Miss Osborne's first grade class at Pershing Elementary about writing in general and writing humor in particular. We will explore the age-old questions "Why bother writing humor?" and "What are you laughing at?" and "Do you really think that's funny?" and "Where did I put my car keys?" We will look into the different types of humor and examine why that is or they are. We'll also examine ways to compile, generate, and rat hole funny material so that when those idiots ask you, "How do you come up with this stuff?" we can smile condescendingly and tell them.

Finally, we will discuss the nuts and bolts of the writing game – Developing your skills as a writer, and how to sell what you write. We might even go into some actual markets where you could possibly sell your wares. I don't mean we'll *physically* go into these places, because… well,

I don't have time to meet with you all individually, but we will go on virtual class field trips, which may or may not require releases signed by your parents. I'll have to check with my lawyer on that. At any rate, I won't guarantee you'll make money on everything you write, but you'll at least have some brochures in your sales bag.

I've been given a lot over the years in my quest to become a writer… mostly a humor writer, so now it's time for me to give something back. Not that I'm any Harry Truman, you understand, or Douglas MacArthur for that matter. It's just that I think I should share with the world what I've learned about writing humor. It's very important to me that you think I have this wonderful altruism, because then you won't think twice about shelling out the price for this book, unless, of course, you found it in Oprah's trashcan, or some such.

Therefore, in the finest tradition of Miss Osborne and all her colleagues who struggled down through the years to get me to quit clowning around and sit down, I want you to spit out your gum, take those pencils out of your nostrils, open your books to Chapter 1, and pay attention.

Are You Serious? Why Write Humor?

"I'd like to be funny," said Alice.

"Chop down fifty trees in the forest," responded the King of Hearts, patting his ample belly.

"Would that make me funny?"

"Oh no, of course not."

"You are not funny."

"Why would I want to be funny?"

"I'm the one who wants to be funny," said Alice with a frown.

"See, you are already becoming funny."

"I'm serious!" Alice stamped her foot.

"Of course," smiled the king...

Alice in Wonderland - Lewis Carroll

If you really want to be a humor writer, you should get used to questions like this:

"Do you ever do any serious writing?"

There are two implications to this question, or those like it. One is the obvious – humor writing is frivolous, and therefore not important writing. The second says, if you're a humor writer, you're somehow second-class to the rest of the literati. We class clowns have always been tolerated for our entertainment value; heck, some people even liked us. But our efforts couldn't be put on the same plateau with those who write romance or mystery or drama or Westerns or… gasp (I'm not worthy, I'm not worthy)… *literary pieces.*

It's like the King of Hearts pointed out to Alice in the literary piece Lewis Carroll wrote (see Satire, later) about a little girl in a ridiculous world – before you can become funny, you need to become serious.

I wrote a literary piece once. I even got a magazine to publish it, and they in turn nominated it for a Pushcart Award. I felt very snooty about that accomplishment for a long time until someone asked me what I got paid for it and I had to tell them two contributor's copies and a nice certificate.

Now I'm not saying you'll get paid a lot for your humor writing, but you'll have a better chance of taking it to the bank than you will a story about a big white whale named Ishmael and a crazy sea captain named Mobile Dick played by Gregory Peck. In fact, humor by itself usually has the following pay scale: Minimum: Nothing; Maximum: Next to Nothing. I ain't (serious writers would never use that word) really going to recommend that you try to become a humor writer in order to make a living. It's good for the pure fun of it, but I recommend writing magazine articles and such, which are in much greater demand, and which pay way better. And remember, not all magazine articles need to be dead serious. Inject your humor skills into them and odds are you'll have a better chance of selling them.

Here's an example of a piece I did for an e-publication on the topic of making money as a writer. It's a humor piece and I made money on it… not much, but it was more than contributor's copies.

How I Made $100 a Year as a Writer

It was 1966. Lyndon Johnson had perfected the sad hound dog look he regularly sent into our homes via Walter Cronkite's evening news, wherein he said (Lyndon, not Walter) something like, "We cannot allow the spread of Comminist agresshun. Therefore, Ah will continyuh to send more young Amurican butts to Vee-et Nam [rhymed with ham], not so much to stop 'em, as to git in thur way."

The spring semester where I attended college had just started, and I was safely protected from LBJ's clutches by a student deferment from the draft.

As an English major, I had to have a certain number of journalism hours to complete my degree and had enrolled in a "Feature Article Writing" class. In the first session, the instructor said, "To make an A in this course, you'll have to write and publish a feature article. That's a *feature,* not some namby-pamby story or poem, so all you English majors who signed up for this class because you think you can write, had better pack up and leave now."

There existed a great dislike between English and journalism majors at that college. Journalism students regarded English majors as effete pseudo-intellectual wimps, and we considered journalism majors as arrogant unkempt bleepheads.

So with two-thirds of the class, I gathered up my things and walked out, not because I didn't think I could write, but because the instructor was an arrogant bleephead. Withdrawing from that class changed my life in two ways: 1 - I missed out on learning skills for writing and selling feature articles, and 2 - by dropping the class, I fell below the minimum requirement to qualify as a full-time student, so LBJ's minions at Selective Service put me on the fast track to the Orient.

Fast-forward twenty-five years. I had rekindled my interest in writing. Had even taken a couple of refreshers on fiction, poetry, and, yes, even feature article writing. I joined local writers' groups and attended conferences. I wrote and wrote and sent stuff out at a semi-furious pace, entered contests, composed queries, synopses, cover letters. I wrote short stories, poems, essays, even a novel. I got many rejections. Once or twice an editor wrote a personal note, some encouraging, others sarcastic (journalism majors, I figured). "Keep trying, don't give up" came the stock reply from instructors and successful writer acquaintances when I whined. So I did.

I offered to write humor columns for local newspapers. A couple accepted, provided I'd do it for free. For three years I did it for free. One year I won a contest for a short story: two hundred bucks. Another year a magazine bought a humor piece I did: fifty bucks. They never published it. Last year I sold an essay to a national magazine, one with a New York address, for ONE HUNDRED - count 'em - AMURICAN DOLLARS! Then they rewrote the whole thing and stuck my name on it.

Based on my observations and experience, here's how I figure you make money writing:

Be a woman.

If you can't be a woman, use a woman's name.

Write gushy romance (this stuff really sells).

Tell editors you're a lawyer or doctor or both (PhD's accepted).

Tell editors you're a woman doctor practicing law. Tell them you're anything but a white guy with a degree in English.

Stay in school and don't take drugs.

Learn to write feature articles.

Don't write humor.

Major in journalism.

Don't offer to write for free.

If offered $100 for something you write that they'll edit beyond recognition, take it.

I threw that piece in here for a couple of reasons. It's free writing I've already done, and this is my book and I can put it in if I want, nyah. And it illustrates several techniques which we will cover in the following chapters. For example, English majors versus Journalism majors. I've already touched on this, but it's worth repeating.

As much as I still strongly dislike Journalism majors, I'll have to admit they have a point. Yes, it's true most of them are snotty and arrogant and uncombed and have horns and vote for Democrats, but when it comes to writing for money they are more better at it than us English majors. (Extra Credit Quiz: There are a couple of English teacher *Where's Waldo*s in that last sentence. Can you locate them? If so, send me your correct answers along with $5 cash and I will send you a nice certificate stating that you done good.)

Journalism majors adhere closely to rules 11 and 12 from the piece above, which essentially say, don't write for free and sometimes you have to swallow your artistic pride, especially if it means paying the electric bill. I hate to admit that makes them smarter than me, but it does on that score.

Again the purpose of this book isn't to tell you how to write magazine articles. There are others, much more qualified than I, to do that. But I do want to emphasize that feature writing and magazine article writing are far more lucrative than just writing your basic humor. There is no law, however, that says you can't include one with the other.

But back to the question about serious writing versus humor writing. Writing humor is very hard and very serious, and if you don't believe that, you're a dope-smoking journalism monkey. Humor is a subjective quality. The ability to write so that your readers find it funny on purpose is not an easy thing to accomplish. It takes practice and keen instincts toward knowing how to use techniques that can generate amusement ranging from a wry smile to falling down, knee-slapping, hiccup-generating, snort-inducing, flatulence-forcing laughter.

Writing humor is a skill developed just as much as that of turning a whale into a metaphor for evil, and a puritanical sea captain into a symbol of your father that spring night when you were a senior in high school, and you came in way late with beer on your breath.

Don't kid yourself… well, you can kid yourself a little if it means you'll write better humor, but what I mean to say is, writing of any kind is hard work. However, writing humor isn't something anybody can do. It's not something every writer can do. There is a certain talent to it, but like that obscure actor who played Robert Redford's dad in *The Natural* said to the young Roy Hobbs, "You really should see somebody about that wart on your face."

No, wait, that was Redford's agent. The line in the movie was, "You have a gift, Roy, but that's not enough."

And just like in baseball, when it comes to hitting and fielding and spitting and scratching your crotch, talent isn't enough. You have to build the skills; you have to develop the craft. Here's where I hope I can help you, by regurgitating on you the meager knowledge I have regarding the subject.

Now I would be the last to admit… I mean, the first to admit… well, no, maybe somewhere in the middle… that I'm no Roy Hobbs when it comes to hitting homeruns at the ballpark of humor; I'm no Sundance Kid when it comes to robbing the banks of laughter; I'm no… whatever his character's name was in *The Sting* when it comes to… uh… I forgot what my point was… Oh yeah, I may not be the definitive source for humor writing knowledge, but I do know some things, I have learned some things, that I don't mind passing along. It's like my psychiatrist says, "Every little bit helps."

What's Funny and Who Cares

Humor Legos

For most of us, writing humor isn't as easy as falling off a log, although that could be very funny if done right (see Pratfalls). We have to have something in our arsenal to call on in order to crank out the funny. There are lots of different types of humor, and what I'm about to discuss certainly isn't a definitive list. They're just the types I could think of and/or (excuse me for that, Professor Strunk) have used myself. The point is, we should look at them to examine how we can write our own brand of humor using some or all of them.

I've arranged these, not so much in the order of their importance as I have alphabetically...more or less.

Anecdotes

These mini-short stories serve to give an account of interesting incidents involving some type of behavior, human or otherwise. They can range from mildly amusing to uproarious, usually delivering a point, but not as a requirement. The best known place to read anecdotes is *Reader's Digest*. They even solicit anecdotes, promising to pay you $100 to $300 for a one hundred word unpublished and true anecdote about work, the military, life in general. You can even submit these on-line now at www.rd.com.

As they say, "everybody has a funny story," so why not write up one of yours and send it to them? If you don't have Internet access (for those of you living in Uptoyerbuttinmudistan), go down to your local Wal-Mart (or equivalent) and buy a copy of the magazine. They tell you where to mail submissions – RD, not Wal-Mart – which editor, etc. But here's a reality check – they get more of these than Wal-Mart has blue bags, so don't fret over one you've sent. Just send it in and fahgidabowdit. And keep sending them.

Here's an example of an anecdote from my past. And by the way, I DID send this in to RD and never heard a peep from them. Maybe it wasn't funny, who knows? No reason to quit trying , though.

> In a battalion headquarters company with the 7th Infantry in Korea, our company's first sergeant was the Yogi Berra of the Army. One hot summer day after we got word that a mechanical inspection was coming down from Division in two days, a hasty company formation was called and Top said, "Okay, I want all uh yuz down to the motor pool right now; the rest uh yuz go back to work."
>
> After several seconds when none of us moved, he said, "Aw right, we're all gonna just stand here in the sun 'til yuz go where I tole ya."

Here's another:

> In Camp Hovey, Korea one morning in 1968 while standing formation for our usual daily announcements, our first sergeant said, "I Corps has been sending us complaints about you people not putting your name and return address on your letters home. From now on if you don't put your return address on your letters, they will be sent back to you."

Here's a suggestion. This is such a good writing exercise, why not make it a goal to create an anecdote every day and submit it to Reader's Digest? Also, remember to keep it at their requirement of one hundred words or less. It's a great way to get in the mental and physical habit and discipline of writing something, and, who knows, some day you might go to your mailbox and pull out a $300 check. But don't do it for the money, do it for the exercise. That way, when a check does come, it will be gravy.

The only drawback to sending these anecdotes in to Reader's Digest is that they don't let you know if they don't want it. If they decide to use it, they'll let you know, but that could be as long as a year. These should be throw-away items in your writing pantry, unless you can find a publication looking for anecdotes and will respond to you within a reasonable time. In that case, send your stories to them first, then on to Reader's Digest if they get rejected.

But if you like lotteries, Reader's Digest is a good place to submit. Approach it with the attitude that it's a writing exercise, and it can be fun.

Burlesque

Now I don't mind looking at scantily clad ladies… Oh, excuse me. That is a way sexist remark, and very inappropriate here. I should be ashamed of myself. Let me re-phrase it.

I don't mind looking at scantily clad *women.*

I know, I know, it's not what you women of the feminist persuasion want to hear, but the fact is, I don't (mind looking). Not that I go around searching for your undressed women to look at, you understand, but if the opportunity presents itself, I look. It's just in my nature as a red-blooded hetero male to do this. I can no more help myself than a bear in the woods can keep from… well, fishing for salmon, for one thing. You take those Victoria's

Secret commercials, for instance… wait… I've gotten distracted here. I'm sorry; this happens. It's a manifestation of the LWS from which I suffer – Lonely Writer's Syndrome. It comes from sitting in front of my computer too long, trying to think of writing topics. I'll talk about that in a later chapter.

When we hear the word *Burlesque*, the first thing that comes to mind for most of us… a lot of us… okay, some of us, is "strip show." That's one definition, but not the main one. Here's what my family dictionary states:

"A literary or dramatic work that makes a subject appear ridiculous by treating it in an incongruous way, as by presenting a lofty subject with vulgarity or an inconsequential one with mock dignity."

Two of your more noted examples of literary burlesque, at least from an English major's view, come from Geoffrey Chaucer and Miguel de Cervantes who wrote *The Canterbury Tales* and *Don Quixote*, respectively. Both of these works ridicule the romance of your medieval times, and Geoffrey made a burlesque of his name which was really Jeffrey. In either case, I suggest you add these two works to your personal library, if you haven't already, so you can get a good idea of how tasteful burlesque should be written.

One word of caution: be sure to get copies in English. *Don Quixote* was originally written in Spanish, and *The Canterbury Tales* in something called "Middle English." That implies, logic would tell you, that there should also be a Left English and a Right English; however, I've never come across either of these, unless you count Phil Donahue and Rush Limbaugh.

In any case, I've got an example of my own attempt at burlesque I'll include here. I don't pretend to be in the same class as Miguel or Geoff, by which I mean my work is required reading for any college freshman, but it's at least written in English. I actually made money on this piece too, but not before it was rejected by a Canadian literary magazine to which I regularly contributed at the time. They considered it too politically incorrect. Bingo! I have written burlesque! But what can you expect. Canadians don't like to read anything not written in either French or Left English. I subsequently sold this to another, less foreign, periodical.

Encyclopedia Trumanica

The other night, during an episode of the news magazine show "Prime 20/48 Minutes", noted smirking reporter Sam Donaldson presented a story about how some of our children's textbooks are filled with inaccuracies, mis-facts, and revisionist entries to satisfy political correctness. "What it boils down to," Sam said smirkingly, "is that the textbook publishers have more interest in selling books than education."

Well, duh, Sam.

Like any concerned American, I reacted with incredulity. "How on earth," I said, "could we as a nation let this happen. And how, as a concerned American, can I cash in on it?"

"Hey," I continued. "If all you gotta do is make things up, I could write my own encyclopedia. I did, after all, major in English." So here's a sample of what I've done so far.

Abaft – toward the stern, as in, "Yo, baby. I couldn't help but notice you've got quite abaft there."

B-girl –Tarzan's shorthand denotation of gender, as in "Me be monkey boy; you b-girl."

Calc-tufa – What the brain matter of your average English major turns into when they mistakenly take a course in calculus.

Calculous – Less severe than calc-tufa. Actual brain calluses resulting from the studying of calculus. Usually only seen on math, engineering, and rocket scientist students, as well as other members of the genus and species nerdae calculatori chessclubus . Rarely seen condition in Liberal Arts majors.

Dacha – German plural of dachshund, meaning two or more wiener dogs.

Edh - A letter appearing in Old Norse to represent an interdental fricative. As in, "Yo Lars, if youse don't gimme the edh youse owe me from your last pillage, I will have Grendel here give youse an interdental fricative."

Facsimile - A figure of speech in which unlike things are compared to something faxed. As in, "These faxes are as clear as calculus problems to an English major." Or, "Dude, these faxes about surfing are, like, awesome."

Great Auk - A large, flightless sea bird (Pinguinus ignoramus) formerly common on northern Atlantic coasts but now extinct. Name is thought to be derived from the sound the creature made right before it was eaten by a shark.

Habakkuk - A Hebrew prophet of the seventh century B.C. Tradition holds that at the prophet's birth, when a hospital scribe asked his parents what they wanted to name the child, his father said, "This boy's name shall henceforth be... be..." Then he sneezed. "Got it," the scribe said writing it down and leaving quickly. Despite his father's laborious efforts in getting the official records changed, young Habakkuk kept the name when he began his prophetable career. In an interview with Barbara Walters during his later years, he said he felt the name would stand a better chance of getting into the Bible than the one his father wanted. "I mean," he said, "who would take me seriously if I was known as The Prophet Bob?"

Ideomotor – Brain mechanism used to prevent stupidity. As in, "Please engage ideomotor before opening mouth."

Idiolect – Children of the 60's who thought smoking dope expanded their minds, and that quoting Kahlil Gibran made them sound smart.

Jason and the Argonauts – A classical Rock 'n Roll group best known for their hit single "Good Goosa, Miss Medusa! You're the Gorgon of my Dreams."

Java Man – Name given to the unusual 700,000 year old fossilized remains of a humanoid skeleton discovered in 1890. It is generally thought scientists came up with this name because they couldn't go around in polite society using its scientific name -Pithecanthropus erectus - for reasons we won't go into.

K–Rations – Survival food you can pick up at K-Mart.

Ka Lahui – a polynesian sneeze

Kahlil Gibran - Lebanese-born American mystic poet best known for wearing flowers in his hair in 1923, smoking funny smelling cigarettes, and writing *The Prophet* - a romantic-comedy musical based on the life of Habukkuk.

Lablab – A place to do experiments experiments

Lacrimae rerum – An early hippy hobby taken from the ancient Jamaican craft of weaving hemp into ugly wall hangings while throwing back several shots of a sugar cane based distillate.

Mabinogion - A collection of Welsh prose tales, composed between the 11th and 13th centuries, but based on an older oral tradition from a galaxy far, far away. Most of the 11 anonymous tales incorporate Welsh mythology and folklore and deal with the Arthurlegend, which later became known as Lucasmania. These stories are preserved in two manuscripts, the White Book of Rhydderch, or the Post Prequel trilogy; and the Red Book of Hergest, or the Big Book of Jedi Megabucks. The first English translation was made from the latter by Lady Fergie Yorkie Porkie, and two decades later re-released with added scenes to suck in the nerdy off-spring of the original members of the brotherhood known as Doofi of the Eternal Star Wars Dorks. You can spot these people today in theaters everywhere nearly wetting themselves during the showing of Episode 1 previews. The meaning of the name Mabinogion is the subject of debate, but only by those who have absolutely no social life. It is derived from the group of four related stories that begins the collection, "The Four Branches of the Mabinogi." Or "Darkside,

Schmarkside. Black Just Happens to be My Color." They concern the life of Prince Gwri or Pryderi or Pfqrstvwx who grows up to be the baddest, heaviest-breathin' villain the world has ever known. This cycle is followed by three independent tales which were developed 20 years before the first creating a paradoxical special effects gap; but, nonetheless, are all totally awesome. The collection concludes with a group of three Arthurian/Lucasian romances, waiting to be funded.

Napolean I (Napolean, the eye) - A brilliant military strategist, he deposed the French Directory (1799) and later, the French Yellow Pages (Nov '02/Oct '03). Soon after (1804) he proclaimed himself The Shortest Emperor in France. His military and political might gripped Continental Europe, but failed to impress Great Britain. During a disastrous winter campaign in Russia, he retreated when, for the first time anywhere, Peter Ilyich Tchaikovsky played his (1812) Overture. Having been exiled to the island of Elba (where he supposedly said, "Able was I ere I saw Elle McPherson.") he became increasingly upset that somebody with a middle name of Ilyich had defeated him, and escaped. He regained power and met Duke Wellington at Watergate (1972). The Napoleonic Code, still forms the basic recipe for French bread.

Oberon – The king of the fairies and husband of Titania in medieval folklore. Not that there's anything wrong with it.

Object Lesson – One of several high school English class sessions on the subject of objects.

Object model – Guest lecturer at an all boys' boarding school, usually in the Cindy Crawford class, brought in to teach object lessons to insure the class members' undivided attention and to get them to sit erect in their seats.

Oblation – The act of something offered to a deity. As in, "After the debate, in which Mars totally kicked Venus' butt, the predominantly male audience, amid fervent shouts of "You da Man!" gave the War Dude a standing oblation.

Black humor

It's important to point out that this category of humor doesn't refer (in these pages, anyway) to humor by or about people of the black race, although there are enough practitioners of the technique for it to be considered a genre all it's own. There are a lot of brilliant individuals who write ethnic humor, but I'm not one of them. For one thing, I'm not qualified. For another, I'm not brilliant. Ethnic humor is just too emotionally charged for me to want to delve into it. I should think writing ethnic humor would best be left to those of that specific ethnicity. I'm only qualified to write ethnic humor of your middle-class Fifty-something Caucasian American male.

On the other hand, humor is humor. All of us, regardless of race, creed, party affiliation, or brand of deodorant have things about us that are funny. Before we start laughing at others, we should first learn to laugh at ourselves. On the topic of ethnic humor, a couple of pertinent momisms bouncing around in my head are – "If you can't say something nice about someone, don't say anything at all," and "I'm not laughing AT you, I'm laughing WITH you." Now I hated it when she said either of these things to me, but they do hold a certain amount of wisdom. Ethnic humor doesn't need to be vicious to be funny. In fact, according to the way I was brought up, that's an oxymoron – viciously funny. By the same token, we need to remember not to take ourselves too seriously in life. We should leave that up to the judgment of the Almighty, or some of His senior management.

All that having been said, let's move on to what we really mean by Black Humor. Maybe a more appropriate name would be Macabre humor – those funny things which deal with death, disease, or suffering in general. All those hilarious things. You write this kind of humor on the premise that there's humor in everything. While there's truth in that, we must remember that just because you think something is humorous, doesn't mean that it's appropriate. There's a time and a place for everything (I hear you, Mom.). Of course, that's where the art of Macabre humor comes in. The feeling that it is inappropriate gives this type of humor it's main ingredient. It's just a very fine line we have to walk so as not to fall over into the territory of bad taste. The writers at SNL (Saturday Night Live) have been doing this for years, often failing, in my opinion, to keep from stirring up the waters of the River Fetid. (Ew, poetic!)

One of the most uproarious and masterful black humor pieces I've ever heard or seen came from a short-lived TV series in the Eighties called *Frank's Place* starring Tim Reid (played Venus Flytrap on *WKRP in Cincinnati*). This sitcom revolved around a Boston college professor who came to New Orleans to take over the restaurant left him by his deceased father. This show only lasted for twenty-two episodes, but it had more good writing in it than ten seasons of *Friends*.

At any rate, one episode entitled (I think) "Where's Ed?" involved three older gentlemen who, after several shots of toasting their recently deceased friend Ed with an adult beverage, decided that he should join them in one last drink. The rest of the episode wound its way through their retrieving Ed, or his remains, from the funeral home and subsequently trying to return him to his casket before the services the next day. I won't go into all the hilarious details of the thirty minute adventure, but it ended with the old guys making it back to the funeral home with Ed in tow, but only getting as far as the back row of the chapel, where they sat down with Ed between them. The service for Ed had started. In the last ten seconds of the episode, after the attendees leave, all except for Ed, of course, the widow goes to the casket to say one last goodbye to her dearly departed. She opens the lid, and finds it empty. She turns around bewildered as if to ask, "Where's Ed?" only to see him sitting on the back row, dressed in black suit, derby and sunglasses, seemingly looking at her. Fade to black.

Now that was macabre humor. Well, maybe you had to see it to appreciate it.

I wrote a short story once using black humor. I won't include it here, because it's about 4,000 words long, but it's based on the old joke about the golfer telling his wife that his lifelong buddy had keeled over dead in the middle of their round that day. "Oh, that must have been awful," the wife exclaimed. And the husband says (punchline), "Oh Lord, yes. It was hit the ball, drag Charlie, hit the ball, drag Charlie."

I had a lot of fun with that story. (Now for some shameless self-promotion) If you want to read it, it's included in my collection of short stories entitled "My Shorts in a Bunch." The story is called "Skins Game." You can find this book at **AWOCBooks.com** in the fiction section. E-book or printed copy.

Jokes/Gags

I find it interesting that one of the meanings of the word gag is joke, while other definitions include the act of choking, and something forced into or put over the mouth to prevent speaking. Some jokes can make us gag, and we should prevent others from ever being told. Perhaps that's how the joke definition of the word gag came about. Something to think about.

Writing jokes is the corner stone of the building blocks at the foundation on the framework of humor writing. It's also the hardest thing to do.

Milt Josefsberg, one of the most prolific and decorated comedy writers in this country, said this about jokes and joke writing: "Jokes, per se, are the cheapest commodity in comedy, and the most necessary... Basically all jokes are constructed the same way. There is the feedline, then the punchline. The feed lineline sets the joke up, the punchline is the snapper that gets the laugh."

Mr. Josefsberg offers this joke as an example in his book *Comedy Writing for Television and Hollywood.* He doesn't say he's the creator, but we'll give him credit here as a contributor. I'll paraphrase it.

> A team of astronauts, a man and a woman, travel to Mars on Earth's first personed exploration. At touch down they are greeted as guests by the Martians and are given a tour of the planet. Eventually they come to a factory which the Martians explain is one of their most advanced baby-making facilities. The Earthlings

watch as a group of workers along a conveyor belt place a lump of clay on it, then another attaches some legs, then another some arms, then a head, nose, eyes, ears, etc. Finally at the end a Martian applies two electronic paddles to give the object a shock and it becomes a squalling, living Martian baby.

The visiting astronauts express their amazement at this method of procreation. The Martians are surprised that Earthlings don't make babies on an assembly line as they do and inquire about the method used on their planet. In the interest of science and interplanetary diplomacy, the Earth man and woman put on a complete demonstration of the human sex act. Now it's the Martians' turn to be surprised.

"That's amazing," says the Martian in charge. "That's the way we make automobiles."

Jokes, as everyone knows, come in all sizes, shapes, and colors. Generally speaking, we rarely know the author or origin of jokes. They just seem to drift in and out of our conversations and social gatherings. They appear to be a part of the public domain. There are, however, good places to find jokes with or without credits due. One of the most abundant is e-mail. Let's see a show of hands from those of you who get at least five forwarded e-mails a day with attached jokes. Now let's see a show of hands of those of you who would like to choke the person or persons who sent you those forwards… Right.

Annoying e-mail aside, the Internet is rife with joke sites. I entered in the word "jokes" in my browser's search feature and got a listing of 635 sites.

Here's good example I found at one site - laughzone.com:

A Rabbi, a Hindu, and a lawyer are in a car. They run out of gas and are forced to stop at a farmer's house. The farmer says there are only two extra beds, so one person will have to sleep in the barn.

The Hindu says, "I'm humble, I will sleep in the barn."

So, he goes out to the barn. In a few minutes, the farmer hears a knock on the door. It's the Hindu and he says, "There is a cow in the barn. It's against my beliefs to sleep with a cow."

So, the Rabbi says, "I'm humble, I'll sleep in the barn."

A few minutes later, the farmer hears another knock on the door and it's the Rabbi. He says that it is against his beliefs to sleep where there is a pig and there is a pig in the barn.

So, the lawyer is forced to sleep in the barn. A few minutes later, there is a knock on the door.

It's the pig and the cow...

Any and everybody can write jokes about any and all things. I can't tell you how many times I've handed a boss or a professor or an arresting officer a report or thesis or alibi on which I spent many hours creating only to have him say, "This is a joke, right?" It really doesn't appear to be that hard. All you need is a set-up and a punchline.

Selling jokes is another matter. There must be a market for writing jokes and gags for comedians, cartoonists, and Rotarians, but I haven't had much success finding out just where or how to do that. The only consistent thing I'm told is that it's extremely competitive. Of course, you could do like I did and start your own cartoon. Actually, Dan Case created Chicken Writer and asked me to write gags for it, so I was lucky. As Dan likes to say, "I'm the chicken, Phil's the writer."

On the other hand, don't let my ignorance stop you. You can't swing a dead cat (or dog, for you cat lovers) in this country without hitting a comedian standing next to a lawyer; and somebody, somewhere must sell them jokes. I can't believe Jay Leno, Jerry Seinfeld, or Hillary Clinton can be that funny on their own.

If you consider joke and gag writing your forte, and you have a bottom drawer full of these, you might try hanging around comedy clubs to try to peddle your jokes to the young comics there. Word has it that's a competitive business, too, and they're always on the lookout for material. They might be willing to pay a buck or two for a few good lines. You could always panhandle outside the door to the club too, as a side enterprise. Hey, if you'd be willing to grovel at the feet of unknown comics, you shouldn't be too proud to do that, either.

And, by the way, if you think you have some good Chicken Writer gags, send them to me and we'll see what we can work out.

A much better place to sell your jokes would be to commercial or trade periodicals. If you don't have a current copy of *Writer's Market* you should invest in one, but only if you don't have a computer and Internet access (Muduptobuttistanians). If you do, subscribe to WritersMarket.com. They charge a yearly subscription rate very much worth the service you get. Frankly, I can't imagine why anyone now-a-days would buy that big, bulky, expensive, hard to manage book Writer's Digest Books puts out every year when you can get virtually the same thing on-line, PLUS the advantage of having a search engine, PLUS regular updates, PLUS having a built-in application that allows you to track your submissions.

If you at least have a computer, but don't have Internet access (Why???), you can buy the book, plus a CD for a rather exorbitant price, I might add. The on-line subscription is much less.

Well, anyway, so much for the free commercial for Writer's Market. But any instructor or advisor on writing for money from kindergarten on will tell you, it's a tool every writer needs to have. So I'm doing my duty too. Let me explain why on the topic of humor writing and joke writing.

I'll wait while you go turn on your computer and log in to WritersMarket.com… Are we there yet?… Yeah, I know it's Windows… *ridin' in my car, listenin' to my ray dio…* Tell you what, why don't we go have some lunch and I'll meet you back here in an hour. You should be up and running by then…

Okay. Man, I love Mexican food. Now, let's get started. If you've signed up and paid your entry fee and you're logged into WritersMarket.com, enter the word "Jokes" in the "search by keyword" field. I got nineteen matches. (humor will get you over 720!) You'll notice that the markets range from trade magazines for the cleaning business to greeting card companies. Most of them want Jokes or short humor from 50 to 100 words and pay anywhere from $1 to $100 for a good joke (or short humor).

Here's something to note. Just because you got a match on the word "joke" doesn't necessarily mean everybody wants you to submit to them. Here's where you should: one – read these guidelines; two – get and read a copy of the periodical to which you want to submit.

Case in point – the *Pacific Bankers News* came back with a match on "Jokes" because they explicitly say, "no jokes." Those bankers out on the Left Coast... What?... Oh, it's *Bakers.* Well, still, they have no truck with us jokesters. There's absolutely nothing funny going on in the baking bidness out there, so don't even try. I guess if you had to get up to bake doughnuts at three in the morning, even if your bakery overlooked the Pacific Ocean, you wouldn't have much to laugh about either. And those brides and their mothers with the wedding cakes!... man, that's enough to take away your sense of humor away right there.

However, there's reason for optimism. Just below the entry for the *Pacific Bakers' News* is a listing for the *Ag-Pilot International Magazine*. A simple double-click on the link shows that this is a "magazine emphasizing agricultural aviation..." What's more important, they will pay up to $10 for jokes, and up to $200 for Nonfiction humor. Now does that cry out for jokes, or what?! I mean, there's got to be at least a dozen Aggie Aviator jokes just dying to be written for this magazine. Agriculture pilots seem to be a much more fun group to work with than Pacific bakers.

So get out there and dig. Your jokes are gold.

Limerick & Light verse

Now here's a category that's really fun to create, but I'm not sure what the market is. I've never sold any humorous verse, although I once won a prize for it at a writers' convention. I do write and have written limericks and haiku for Chicken Writer. Here's some examples:

One of the Chicken Writer characters is a Mule who sits under a tree and writes haiku on his laptop. We call it Mule Haiku:

(this one is decidedly political)

Seeking greener grass
Frenchman asks my Donkey's game
He should kiss my ass.

Horse fly bites my back
Shivering hide snorting protest
Mule life is no fun.

Leather reins slap my back
He Shouts gee and haw and git
And I will not move.

Pigs wallow in mud
Oinks and grunts mean happy hogs
The stink rises in June.

And then there are the limericks:

There once was a bull named Ellington
Whose beef against beef was quite eloquent
But he crossed over the bar
Took his protest too far
And got served up as medium rare Wellington.

There once was an owl from Vancouver
Whose spots made her one famous hooter
Environmentalists adored her
Their protection they'd award her
But Chuck Heston would just as soon shoot her.

Here's a neat poem that fits into the category of light verse. I want to include it here because it does two things: It's humorous light verse, and it's writer instructive. Thanks to fellow humor writer Debbie Haskins from Denton, Texas for giving me permission to share it with you:

A Love Affair with Adverbs

By Debbie Haskins

She wanted to write a great novel.
She wanted to make it alive.
But drowning in copious adverbs
Her story may not survive.

Did Maxwell the hero move quickly?
Perhaps she should say he was swift
While holding a gaily wrapped present
Or clutching a birthday gift?

Is Charlotte exceedingly tiny
Or skinny without any bust?
Does Maxwell gaze longingly at her
Or stare with unhidden lust?

The weather was terribly sultry.
Or was it a scorching heat wave?
And will Charlotte's father frown fiercely
Or wear an expression grave?

Did truly and madly their love burn
Or was it a fire of the heart?
And desperately will they be leaving
Or deep in the night depart?

Eventually should they be parents
Or bring forth a handsome strong boy?

And do they live happily after
Or treasure an endless joy?

To adverb or not plagued our writer
Who thought that they had a nice ring.
So each one she lovingly cherished
And never published a thing.

Several of those joke listings we looked up on WritersMarket.com listed light verse and haiku as a want, except, of course, the Pacific Bakers. Even the Ag-pilots people want humorous light verse, as long as it relates to Aggie aviation. Well, I should think so. That alone should be limerick rich country. And they'll pay you up to fifty bucks.

Contrary to popular belief, there is money to be made in poetry – humor poetry.

One-liners/Quips/Quotes

You would think these could fall into the Jokes/Gags category, and to some extent they do, but they have a subtle difference.

The traditional joke runs about 50 to 250 words, and has the set up and punch line elements.

The Quip, or one-liner, is a clever, witty, usually sarcastic remark often prompted by the occasion, but not always. It can have the elements of a joke.

The Quote can be a quip, but is attributed to an individual, although sometimes the quip of the quoted individual is anonymous. Of course, the easiest way to tell a quote from a quip is that quotes usually have quotation marks around them.

Got that? Okay, here's some examples of quips and quotes. These first two are quips or one-liner jokes from comedian Stephen Wright whose droll sense of humor and deadpan delivery has delighted many:

> One morning my girlfriend asked me if I slept well and I replied "No, I made a few mistakes."
>
> When I was a baby I kept a diary. Recently, I was re-reading it. It said: Day 1: Still tired from the move. Day 2: Everybody talks to me like I am some kind of idiot.

Quoted quips most often come from people who intend to be funny. Some quotes, however, are hilarious because the quoter was dead serious. Back during the Bush 41 era, Dan Quayle provided a plethora of quotes, but Yogi Berra is still the King of Quotes.

Here's some:

> Vice President Dan Quayle –
>
> "A low voter turnout is an indication of fewer people going to the polls."
>
> "We're going to have the best-educated American people in the world."
>
> "What a waste it is to lose one's mind. Or not to have a mind is being very wasteful. How true that is."

Then I ran across these quotes from super models on laughzone.com:

> ON HEREDITY
>
> "My husband was just OK looking. I was in labor and I said to him, 'What if she's ugly? You're ugly.'"—Beverly Johnson
>
> ON INNER STRENGTH

"I love the confidence that makeup gives me."—Tyra Banks

ON LOGIC

"I think, If my butt's not too big for them to be photographing it, then it shouldn't be too big for me."—Christy Turlington

And, of course, The Yog-meister:

"You can observe a lot by watching."

[When asked the time] "You mean now?"

Okay, so I gave you some pretty good quips and quotes, but so what? Is there any money to be made from quips and quotes, you may ask? My answer may be, I don't know. But they can be funny. Once again, Reader's Digest will pay for quotes from contemporary people. They'd have to be rare, though. Most likely all the Dan Quayle quotes have been submitted at one time or another. And, of course, Yogi Berra has his own e-store. With a quarter of a million submissions a year to RD, unique quotes may be hard to find. You might try garage sales.

Parody

The definition of this writing technique is very close to that of burlesque, so just go back to the section on burlesque if you want a definition. Burlesque can be parody, but not all parody is burlesque. More importantly, we must ask ourselves, so what. This is a rhetorical question; therefore, I didn't use a question mark, which is perfectly legal in most states.

Parody is one form of humor that seems to be in great vogue. Maybe that's because there's so much to parody in today's world, or maybe it's because it has always been in vogue and I just didn't pay attention when they came to that part in my literature classes.

The most abundant contemporary parody, and sometimes some of the best, comes from the writers at the long-running TV comedy show, Saturday Night Live. Other's I think of are the Mel Brooks movies, now classics, which parody movies – *Blazing Saddles* (westerns), *Young Frankenstein* (horror), *Space Balls* (Sci-Fi, particularly the *Star Wars* series). Brooks's parodies were heavily accented with burlesque. And, more recently, the outrageously hilarious *Austin Powers* series which parody (with burlesque) the James Bond type spy films of the '60's and '70's.

I'm sure some of you out there reading this book could write for Saturday Night Live, and perhaps there's another Mel Brooks amongst you. The challenge is getting you discovered. And while literary parody is a good and fun thing to do, your best bet at selling this type of writing would be through the entertainment industry, vis a vis, an agent. Finding and getting an agent to represent you is a whole other book. Unfortunately, I'm not the expert to write that one, either.

On the other hand, there is one magazine whose name is virtually synonymous with parody and satire and is 100% freelance written – *Mad Magazine.* This venerable rag (1952) is "always on the lookout for new ways to spoof and to poke fun at hot trends." The only catch is, you need to have some cartooning ability. They don't look at much that isn't visual.

Sophomoric/Bathroom Humor

This is your burping, farting, pooping, peeing, vomiting and other bodily functions category of humor. It gets its laughs from the shock or surprise value and the inappropriateness of it. For example, I'll bet most of you had a sense of discomfort when you read the first sentence above, and some of you probably expressed that discomfort by giggling. I suppose there's a market for this kind of wit, but I don't personally indulge in it much. Still, people between the mental ages of ten and fifteen really seem to like it. (See "*Dumb and Dumber*.")

Here's a column I wrote using sophomoric funniness, although it's not one of my prouder moments in humor writing.

Humor Gimmes

WARNING. This column contains material that may be too intense for some namby pamby readers. You know who you are, and you should now go to some other dot.com of a milder nature, such as www.MarthaStewart.flowerpots. WithRibbons.andStuff.com. Puritanical discretion is advised.

Today's lesson on humor will deal with some of what's known in the trade as Humor Gimmes. Humor Gimmes - or HG's - are words, sights, and sounds that are automatically funny. That is, you see it, hear it, say it, make it and laughter is instant and spontaneous.

We experience humor through only three of our senses - seeing, hearing, and writing. Rarely do we find humor in taste or feel or smell. Something can feel or smell funny but usually not to the point of producing laughter. When we do experience humor in taste, it's usually bad; however, that doesn't mean it isn't funny. For example, certain bodily noises when emitted will cause us to laugh like dolts, but they are always in bad taste. These noises are known in scientific circles as flatulosity, but are commonly referred to by the – I'll spell it out for those of you who are parents – f-a-r-t word. Regardless of what you call them, they can be catagorized into several categories. In this session we will only deal with the most common.

The Grreeeepop - Usually performed by a grandmother type. She will discharge it discreetly, and totally ignore stares in her direction as if it most certainly didn't happen. Laughter to the observers comes in suppressed giggles and blue faces.

The Frip-frip-fffrrrap-frip - Anyone can produce this one, but it usually comes from moms hurrying down the hallway on a mission. Everyone in the household hoots.

The Booompcusssssh - These are reserved for grandfathers, fathers, and assorted uncles and are released intermittently during the watching of sporting events. Brings on grunting laughter from the rest of the male grouping.

The KeeEEERRRRRrrrup - Performed by teen-aged boys trying to impress their peers. Resulting commotion is much like that following the release of a python in a monkey house.

The Perrrrrrrp - Produced by royalty or ladies of great dignity such as Queen Elizabeth or Martha Stewart. Laughter is only permitted in the House of Commons or servants quarters and certainly not in the presence of the one who dealt it.

The BRAKABRAKABRROOOM - From men 25-65 usually when they're shaving in the morning. Not much laughter due to small audience in attendance. The perpetrator will break out in giggles. The dog just gets up and leaves the room.

Another common Humor Gimme is the wiener dog. No one, except possibly Al Gore, can look at a wiener dog and not laugh like a funhouse clown on nitrous oxide. Throughout history wiener dogs have been used to bring levity to otherwise tense situations. In fact, that's originally what they were bred for in Germany where they're official name is *der Vienerhund*. Wars have been averted using wiener dogs. In 1809, Napolean's army was about to invade Australia when they were met at the border by a host of charging wiener dogs. The usually blasé French soldiers couldn't keep from falling down laughing when they saw the sight. This is known in some history books as the Battle of the Franks and Grey Poupon.

The last Humor Gimme we'll discuss certainly qualifies as an HG, but it's rather disturbing. It's called Men Getting Hit in the Crotch. This has only materialized as an HG in the last couple of decades with the advent of those TV home video shows. Apparently it's an FCC regulation that these shows can't be aired unless they have at least one clip of some poor dude taking a crotch hit by a bat, a ball, a kite, a boomerang, a golf club, a croquet mallet, a karate kick, a Disney character, or a Douglas fir tree. Admittedly, it is funny, but I've noticed guys always have a pained look and grab themselves when they laugh; whereas, women call for re-plays.

> We've briefly touched on what many consider to be the Big Three HG's. There are many, many more but I just can't think of them right now. You'll have to excuse me. For some reason my pants just fell down.

Finding markets for this category of humor shouldn't be too hard. I searched for "sophomoric humor" on my 'Net browser and came up with 5,832 links. It appears most of these are individual sites with individual contributions. Of course, I only looked at about twelve, seven of which had cartoons or jokes involving zits. Conclusion: sophomoric humor is written mainly by sophomores.

Puns/ Malaprops/Word-Play

I've never heard anyone say they hate puns. Despite the fact they're billed as the lowest form of humor, and people cringe when they read or hear them, puns are very popular. Malaprops, a close cousin to puns, aren't as popular, but they're my personal favorite.

The Malaprop was invented in 1775 by British playwright Richard Sheridan when he had one of his characters in the play *The Rivals,* mangle the language. He did such an effective job with Mrs. Malaprop that the word has become a part of our language. Yes, despite a strong feminist influence over the past twenty years or so to supplant it with the word "Ms." (pronounced "miz"), the word "Mrs." (pronounced "mizrus") still owns a prominent place in our language.

I ran across a little book of puns published in 1968 which is a treasure trove of the little devils (puns). Here's a couple of excerpts. Seeing as how this is a book on writing, I stuck with those having a literary theme:

(As the voice of Chicken Writer, this is my favorite)

A novelist confided to friends that he had acquired [some] chickens and wanted names for them. [There came] the following suggestions: Macduff; Chickov; Eggtha Christie; Henny VIII; Shelly; Gregory Peck; Gizzard of Oz; Himalaya...; Fryer Tuck; Ku Klux...; and Brooders Karamazov.

A remarkable character named Alamany has compiled these literary notes:

Mark Twain wrote a book about what his hero would do when his best friend died – Huck'll Bury Finn.

Sir Walter Scott wrote about the occupation of the Russian farmer – Ivan Hoe.

J.D. Salinger wrote about what would happen if a husband came home and found his wife in a tub of whiskey – Catch Her in the Rye.

And the best seller of them all tells us what the cow said when her gentleman friend was leaving the pasture – "Bye, Bull."

As luck would have it, this very morning I happened upon my very own pun. I'd walked into the kitchen to re-fill my coffee cup when my wife started talking to me about a continuing education course she was taking on fibromyalgia (she's a massage therapist).

"All of our muscles, organs, and other body structures are surrounded by connective tissue called 'fascia,'" [pronounced fash-uh] she explained un-solicited.

I couldn't stop myself. "So, you could say all of us are fascia plates?"

The best use of malaprops came from the old TV series *All in the Family* and it's crustaceous main character Archie Bunker played by the late Carroll O'Connor. A few that I recall: Archie telling someone that Edith (his wife) was acting weird because she was going through "mental pause." Archie's referring to a gynecologist as a "groinocologist." And saying that his hasty reactions were "done on the sperm of the moment."

Word-play pretty much goes hand in hand with puns and malaprops, but can stand alone pretty much on its own too. Everybody knows about Abbott and Costello's *Who's on First* routine, and it's got its own alcove in the comedy hall of fame, but one of the best examples of word-play is from the old Danny Kaye movie *The Court Jester*. Every once in a while I'll catch this film on a "classics" channel. If you've never seen it, it's worth checking to see if it's available at your local Blockbuster.

The movie is set in medieval times, and Kaye is about to do battle with a very big and scary knight. Of course, it's a mistake that he's in that position to begin with so he gets help from a couple of women in the castle. One of the women, Griselda, informs Kaye she has put something in one of the drinks the two combatants will toast with, so he has nothing to fear as long as he gets the right drink. This is known (at least, be me) as the "Vessel in the Pestle Scene," and it goes like this:

Griselda: Listen. I've put a pellet of poison in one of the vessels.

Kaye: Which one?

Griselda: The one with a figure of a pestle.

Kaye: The vessel with the pestle?

Griselda: Yes, but you don't want the vessel with the pestle, you want the chalice from the palace.

Kaye: I see. I want the chalice from the – what?

Jean (impatiently): The chalice from the palace.

Kaye: Hmm?

Griselda: A little crystal chalice with a figure of a palace.

Kaye: But does the chalice with the palace have the pellet with the poison?

Griselda: No, the pellet with the poison is in the vessel with the pestle.

Kaye: The pestle with the vessel?

Jean: No—the vessel with the pestle!

Kaye: What about the palace from the chalice?

Griselda (sternly): Not the palace from the chalice, the *chalice* from the *palace*!

Kaye: And where's the pellet of poison?

Gris: In the vessel with the pestle.

Jean (impatiently): Don't you see? The pellet with the poison's in the vessel with the pestle. The chalice from the palace has the brew that is true. It's so simple, I can say it.

Kaye: Then *you* fight him.

Gris: Now listen carefully. The pellet with the poison is in the vessel with the pestle; the chalice from the palace has the brew that is true.

There's an interlude where Griselda leaves Kaye while he practices the above line, screwing it up many times until he finally gets it right at which point he approaches Griselda and proudly says: The pellet with the poison is in the vessel with the pestle; the chalice from the palace has the brew that is true.

Griselda (frantically): No, no. There's been a change.

Kaye: What???

Gris: They broke the chalice from the palace.

Kaye: Oh, no.

Gris: And replaced it with a flagon.

Kaye: A flagon??

Gris: With a figure of a dragon.

Kaye: The flagon with a dragon?

Gris: Yes.

Kaye: But did you put the pellet with the poison in the vessel with the pestle?

Gris: No. The pellet with the poison's in the flagon with the dragon. The vessel with the pestle has the brew that is true...

Classic funny, right? Right. There's plenty of room for puns and word play in your humor writing, if it's done write. One of the best places for puns and wordplay is in cartoons. I use them abundantly in Chicken Writer.

There are pun sites you can visit to explore the puns of others. A couple of the better ones I've located are PunsGalore.com and PunOfTheDay.com. If you're so inclined, they'll even take submissions. I could not find, however, anything to indicate they would pay you anything for your efforts other than recognition.

Satire/Lampoon

This category of writing employs humor in the form of irony, innuendo, sarcasm, caustic wit, or outright derision to lay bare human foolishness. Lampoon is a broader satirical piece that ridicules a person, group, or institution. Some of the best imitates the characteristic style of an author or work for comic effect.

Here's an example of one of my attempts at sat*ire.* This selected short is from my book of collected short stories entitled, *My Shorts in a Bunch.*

A Brief History of Programming

Late in 1939, in Dodge City, Kansas, Professor Marvin "The King Dweeb" Univac finished building the world's first electronic computer.

"What's that thing?" Marvin's wife Myrna had asked him as she handed him a sack of groceries.

She had just pulled up in the driveway, having come from the supermarket. Standing next to the car with the back door open, she'd already shouted, "Hey!" to him as he sat on some old paint cans by the garage door admiring his handiwork and ignoring her. "Could I *please* get some help here?" she wanted to know in an exasperated, and not altogether un-sarcastic, tone. His reverie broken, he jumped up, grinning like some half-witted undergrad, and trotted over to help her carry in the groceries.

"That, my dear, is an electronic computing machine," he said with much pride.

"A what?"

"You know, a computer."

"Uh-huh. What does it do?"

"Well, it... it... Oh, all sorts of things. It's mainly for solving big problems and stuff. I haven't quite got that part figured out yet."

"Marvin, did you fix the toilet like I asked you?"

"Uh, not yet, I—"

"What about the gutters. Have you cleaned those out yet?" She looked up at the roof's edges. "Nooo, I guess not. And I see the screen door is still not fixed. Oh, and look at those leaves. Why I bet they haven't been raked and burned yet, either. But, that's okay. We can do all that later. Right now we have to build a... what did you call it?"

"A computer."

"...a *computer* that will solve big problems."

The computer sat in his garage untouched for eighteen months until his wife told him to either make it do something useful or get rid of it. So Marvin put this ad in the Kansas City Star's Sunday classified section:

NOW HIRING

Ground floor opportunity in the exciting new field of computer nerdology. Two entry level position available. Applicants must possess a working knowledge of geek related activities, such as, laughing loudly at inappropriate times, putting white tape on your glasses, wearing glasses, reading copious amounts of science fiction. Requires as much knowledge and skill in science and electronics as your tormentors on the football team had in making bodily noises. Benefit package includes company paid bad haircuts, multi-colored ink pens, and various small pocket-sized screwdrivers. Must provide reliable plastic pocket liner. Send resumes with salary history to...

Professor Univac received over seven resumes, and narrowed it down to three finalists: Frances "Icky" Cobol, George Frederick "The Fredster" Fortran, and Robert "Space Cadet" Goddard. Cobol and Fortran won the jobs, but Marvin had to pass on Goddard. No contest on his brilliance and nerd-ability, but all he wanted to do was launch the computer into outer space.

"I want you boys to come up with a language my computer here can understand," Univac said to his new assistants. "I figure we've got six months at the most before the little woman turns it into scrap for the war effort. So let's get to work."

Cobol and Fortran worked night and day for several months, but made no progress. They tried Spanish, Swedish, Russian, Yemen, Uzbecki, Turkmeni, Afgani, British, French, Italian, and Thousand Island, but nothing got through to the brooding hulk of a computer.

Word spread of their endeavors, and folks gathered from as far away as Wichita to sit outside the garage on those hot sultry Kansas nights to watch the three men trying to get the computer to respond.

One hot moonlit night, a small freckled-face boy approached the tired and dejected trio.

"Hey, mister," he said. He held up the end of a power cord to Marvin. "Maybe if you plugged this thing into the wall..."

The three computer professionals, sweat glistening their faces and soaking their shirts in the hot and humid night air, looked at one another for several seconds without saying anything. The only sound came from the singing of the crickets in the hot sweltering summer night. Finally Fortran grabbed the plug from the boy and jammed it into a nearby electrical outlet.

"We knew that," he said brusquely to the lad.

The metal and glass behemoth sparked and glittered to life. A great cheer went up from the perspiring crowd gathered on the edge of the garage light's hot yellow glow. Then silence fell as Cobol stepped to the machine and placed his hands on the console. After a brief pause, his fingers raced across the keyboard.

"Swahili," he said hoarsely to his colleagues.

"Swahili," the whisper ricocheted through the hopeful heat-worn crowd.

The machine ground and whirred and blinked, while Vanna and the crowd applauded. "Come on Vegas Trip," Fortran said aloud, his face glazed with sweat and greed. Then it stopped.

Everyone leaned forward expectantly. "Ooooohh," they said. Univac walked to the side of the machine kicking it soundly, and it flashed to life again. "Aaaaahh," said the crowd.

"Ptui," it replied. A piece of paper ejected from its crude output port. Cobol retrieved it, looked at it briefly, frowned, and shook his sweat-dripping head.

The scientists slumped. "Oooooohh," said the well-heated gallery again, as if the Great Wheel had stopped on "Bankrupt."

The disconsolate head geek sank to a chair and stared darkly at the baked dirt floor. Cobol began listlessly throwing damp clothing and his back issues of *Weird Stories for the Scientifically Inclined* into his canvas travel bag. Fortran shuffled about aimlessly with his hands in his pockets, and began to bang his head slowly and repeatedly on the side of the indifferent computer. The crowd began to disperse in twos and threes into the hot muggy night.

On the very edge of the garage's golden light, in swirling ground fog backlit by a blue-white light, stood the silhouetted figure of a man sitting astride a Harley. He stood taller than Paul Newman or Richard Dreyfus, and bore a striking resemblance to Kevin Kostner. With his cold, steel-blue eyes hooded by the bill of his snap-brimmed cap, no one could tell he was a man who had never known the meaning of defeat. With the back-lit blue-white light and swirling fog obscuring his countenance, none there could tell he also didn't know the meaning of ubiquitous nor mnemonics nor pteridology, to name but a few.

In one fluid movement he dismounted the big bike and strode forward into the light. As he walked his unbuttoned, ankle-length canvas coat flowed out from his body like an unbuttoned ankle-length canvas coat. Dust and fog swirled in his wake like dust on a hot dusty summer night in Kansas. Is was so hot, dusty and sultry, it resembled a beer commercial, except the women had on more clothes.

Doc Univac looked up at the stranger standing silently before them. "Howdy, stranger," he said cautiously.

The Stranger touched a forefinger to the bill of his cap and nodded slightly. His blue-green eyes were kind of squinty because of the dust, and sweat rivuleted down his cheeks because of the heat.

"You're a stranger around here, aintcha Stranger?" the wary Fortran asked.

"Could be," came the Stranger's vigilant reply.

"What's yer bidness in these parts, Stranger?" Cobol asked cautiously with wary vigilance.

"I heard a voice. I believe it was a Sioux voice coming from a vast ocean. It said, 'If they build it, you oughta go take a look-see.' It said you boys was in trouble. It said I should come give you a hand."

"Well now, don't that beat all," the sarcastic Fortran said sarcastically. "This here peckerwood thinks we need his hep."

The crowd, which had started to re-form when the blue-white back light and fog had been switched on, laughed derisively. More than a few of them mentioned the heat.

"Hold on there, Fredster," Doc Univac said as he clamped a crooked little cigar between his teeth. "Let's see what this stranger's got in mind." He swiped a match across his pant leg and lit the crooked little cigar. Holding the burning match a few inches from his sweaty beard-stubbled face so that you could see the flame's yellow reflection in his pupils, he said, "Go ahead, Stranger. What ya got in mind."

The stranger's greenish-hazel eyes met Doc's stare evenly. He slowly removed his ankle-length canvas coat, and walked calmly over to the console. "What you boys have failed to understand," the Stranger said as he placed his large rough fingers onto the keyboard, "is that this machine ain't human. It's a machine."

He began to type, slowly at first then with increasing speed and intensity. Sweat poured down the side of his face, and into his intense brown eyes which he blinked away. Dark wet circles grew on his shirt under his arms. The sound of clicking keys began to drown out the chirping of the hot night's crickets, which caused them to file a grievance with the United Swarmhood of Noisome Insects.

Finally, the sweating stranger stopped. "There now," he said. "Let's see what we got. Someone ask it a question."

A murmur went up from the crowd.

"Wh-What's your name?" Doc Univac asked tentatively.

The Stranger keyed in the question, and the great machine blinked and clicked and whirred. Then it spit out an answer.

The Stranger picked up the output and read the response. "I am Univac 1, but you can call me 'U'."

A gasp went up from the crowd. Small Picket signs went up from the crickets.

"Who is the President of the United States?" asked Fortran.

"Franklin Theodore Roosevelt," came the reply.

"What's the square root of 144?" asked Icky Cobol.

"Thirteen, no Twelve, no Thirteen... wait, twelve," U burped out immediately.

The crowd erupted into excited crowd noise. A woman fainted; another screamed. "It's an abomination!" someone yelled. Pitchforks and torches were brandished. The entire third shift of crickets walked off the job.

Then one of the crowd's number, a simple farmer, stepped out of the crowd and approached the scientists, his simple straw hat in his hands.

"Sir? Doctor Univac, sir?"

"Yes, what is it?" Univac said with irritation.

"Kin I mebbe ask it a question?"

"Okay, go ahead. But be quick about it."

"Well, I was wonderin', if it ain't too much trouble..."

"Come on, man. Ask your question."

"Okay, uh, well," he paused and scratched the side of his head. "I was wonderin'... Is the conjugate of the quotient of two conjugate numbers equal to the quotient of their respective conjugates, or what?"

All eyes turned to the Stranger. The Stranger keyed in the question. The massive computer groaned and belched forth its answer. The Stranger pulled it out and read it in silence.

"Well?..." asked Cobol. "What does it say?"

"Yo mamma," the Stranger read.

And so it went through the remainder of the night. Finally, as the sun began to crest over the eastern hills, the Stranger put on his coat and hat and long canvas coat, which he left open so it could flow when he walked, and prepared to leave. The crickets working the first shift began arriving in their tiny pickups, but none of them crossed the picket lines.

"Looks like I've done everything I can here. You boys can handle it now. Just take it easy for awhile 'til he gets used to you. Adios, amiga." With that the Stranger mounted his Harley and rode away to play golf with dolphins in Sherwood Forest.

"Who was that stranger," Cobol asked no one in particular.

"Don't you know?" said one of the hot dusty and, by now, smelly farmers. "Why that's the Lone Assembler."

Not everyone knows this story of how computer programming began, because not everyone watches the Discovery Channel. To be honest, this story hasn't ever actually been told on the Discovery Channel, but that doesn't mean it couldn't happen.

In 1982, the aged Professor Univac attended a dinner at the White House to honor Admiral Grace Hopper for her contribution to computer science, and Steve Jobs for what he brought to the world of suspenders. After the venerable geek Univac had related this story to President Reagan, the Great Communicator looked at the professor and said, "Well, could you pass the mashed potatoes, please?"

Two of the best-known sources for satire are *Mad Magazine* and *National Lampoon,* both of which say they will accept submissions. Submission guidelines can be found on their respective websites: madmagazine.com and nationallampoon.com.

National Lampoon, which was created by Harvard students in 1979, will allow you to submit things on-line, but not before you read and sign a long legalistic "Submission Agreement," presumably written by Harvard law students. They don't really say how, when, or how much they'll pay.

Mad will pay you moderately big bucks if they buy your submissions; however, the competition is fierce and the standards high (another oxymoron). Mad is traditionally a visual magazine, so your submissions should include a visual concept, if not accompanying artwork.

Sight Gags/Cartoons

By definition a sight gag doesn't' get a laugh from written words, but the addition of one-liners or scripts can have a synergistic effect.

Obviously, sight gags only show up in places where you can see them (No! You think?) such as movies, TV shows, and cartoons - animated or static. The "Airplane" movies, the aforementioned Mel Brooks films, those Charlie Sheen spoofs - *Hot Shots* and *Hot Shots Part Deux* – are treasure troves of sight gags. Who can forget the dead Aunt Edna (the late Imogene Coca) strapped to the top of the Family Truckster in National Lampoon's *Vacation*, or the Chihuahua in all the places Charlie Sheen went to sit in *Hot Shots*, or Mongo (Alex Karras) in *Blazing Saddles* punching out a horse, or the blow-up auto-pilot doll in *Airplane*.

But this book isn't about making movies. It could maybe be about writing for movies, but I'm not exactly sure how you write a sight gag. If you're a cartoonist, on the other hand, you can create sight gags ala Gary Larsen (The Far Side) or Berkeley Breathed (Bloom County) or Phil Truman (Chicken Writer)… oh, yeah, Dan Case helps with Chicken Writer. Technically, every cartoon is a sight gag.

Now I'm not saying I'm in the same class as Larsen and Breathed. I'm not saying, mind you, I could create something as funny as Wiener Dog Art, but then again, I'm not saying I couldn't.

You too could become a famous cartoonist or write gags for one. Don't worry about being able to draw. Case in point – Scott Adams and Dilbert. If your gags are funny enough, the art don't matter much… no offense, Dan.

There are many solicitations for cartoon gag writers in various periodicals found in *Writer's Market*. And the greeting card companies are always looking for a few good people to write gags. If you can break in with them, they pay pretty well, too.

Let's talk a little about cartoon gags. These are first cousins – or kissing cousins, if you're from Arkansas – of your one-liners or quips we discussed earlier.

Cartoon gags are surprisingly hard to write… for me, anyway. Dan really helps me with these in Chicken Writer. He'll suggest a situation with the characters in a roughed out panel, and I'll think up what they might say. We depend a lot on themes. Because CW is mainly a cartoon for writers, our gags revolve around situations that are near and dear to writers – writing articles, novels, op/ed, getting rejections, getting acceptances, getting rejections, writers' groups, and getting rejections. But not always.

Sometimes I can't help myself and put in some political stuff. The only problem with that is they don't have much staying power. They're quickly dated. To quote Gene Shalit, "There's hardly anything sadder than humor past its prime." When we come out with our Chicken Writer calendars, we'll have to omit those. Still, there's absolutely nothing wrong with writing (and drawing) political cartoons as long as you have a ready and current market in which to distribute them.

Here's a few examples of one-liners I've used in Chicken Writer. The first couple demonstrate a running theme we have. We thought the Chicken Soup books were good business for our writers, but Chicken Writer had an aversion to writing Chicken Soup bits, so she came up with *Veggie Soup for the Chicken's Soul.* With these we incorporated several humor writing techniques – parody, satire, quips:

Chicken Writer
(c) 2003 AWOC.COM
by Dan Case &
Phil Truman
Veggie Soup for the Chicken's Soul
Golden are the kernels of corn thrown by the farmer's wife.
http://WWW.AWOC.COM/ChickenWriter

Chicken Writer
(c) 2003 AWOC.COM
by Dan Case &
Phil Truman
Veggie Soup for the Chicken's Soul
The delight in finding grub worms is only scratching the surface.
http://WWW.AWOC.COM/ChickenWriter

Here's an example of sight gags and word play and one with a little politic opinion thrown in:

Way back in the halcyon days of yore – about 1992 – Dan and I did a comic strip called *A Whole Other Country* which took a look at the wit and wisdom of the redneck side of Texas and Oklahoma, of which we're both a part. Although it was one of the best things we ever did, in my humble opinion, we never did succeed in selling this strip or getting it syndicated. No shame there, however. Selling and syndication of a comic strip is competitive beyond description.

Be that as it may, I wanted to include a few of these panels as examples of some of the humor techniques we've discussed.

By the way, for you trivia buffs, the acronym AWOC, which has identified the domain of the award-winning E-zine Writing for DOLLARS! related sites for years, comes from the title of this strip.

This panel uses a sight gag and wordplay (Tyson the boxer and Tyson Chicken)

We introduced a character named Joan Peta so we could parody environmentalist, animal rights, feminist left-wing liberals (to counter our rednecks). As a sight gag we decided to always surround her with forest creatures ala Snow White. Here you see the two main characters, Punch

– the one with the moustache – and Whitey in their initial confrontation with her.

Writing gags for a comic strip presents some special challenges. You have to think small and tight. The dialogue has to be brief enough so as not to take away from the artwork, but at the same time able to communicate your set-up and punch line.

If you're both cartoonist and gag writer it's a little easier to work out the logistics and layout of a strip. Fortunately, Dan and I had a good system between us. I could conceive of a gag and write up the dialogue. As I did so, I'd write it in the format of a screenplay, naming the characters, blocking out their actions, movements, emotions, and expressions; then Dan would draw it up like a storyboard… which, when you get right down to it, is what a comic strip is. And to much the same extent, we follow the same procedures with Chicken Writer. It works out well for us.

What I'd do with AWOC is think up a scenario, sort of a mini-sitcom episode, then break it down into gags of four panels each. Depending on the involvement of the situation, I could easily come up with a series of two to five four panel gags. The two strips above and below are examples of that. We did a series on garage sales which went on for about ten strips.

These two panels are a little dated now, but they came out shortly after the movie "Twister" hit the theaters. As long time residents of Tornado Alley, where the action in this movie supposedly took place, we had plenty of material to make some sardonic observations about the attitude elitist Hollywood types have about us Heartland simpletons. It's like the scene I saw in a movie where this Tom Cruise hot shot (it may have been Tom Cruise) approaches a whittling rube sitting on a bench outside a small town barber shop, smirks at him and says, condescendingly, "Whatcha whittlin' old timer?" To which the "old timer" looks up at him with disdain and says, "A grand piano. What does it look like."

To some extent, strips are much easier to write than single panel toons. You can stretch out what you want to say a little more. With single panels the setup, delivery, and punch line have to be contained in one or two relatively short sentences. You have to allow SOME room for the art work… I guess.

In either case, gag writing for cartoons or strips is a very good exercise in learning the skills of precision and brevity in humor writing. I would highly recommend giving this element a try. If you're lucky enough to find an artist with the gift for cartooning like I was, all you have to do is write and block the gags. If you have the talent yourself, the up side is you won't have to split the buckets of money you'll take in, and you probably won't have differences of opinion with yourself over what's fit to create. The down side is, you'll have to do all the work.

Mining the Diamond Fields of Humor

Drink Up Humor Daily With or Without Meals

Remember the old (1980) ribald classic movie *Caddy Shack*? One of the most quoted lines, and this movie has several, came from the playboy Zen-istic golfer played by (a young) Chevy Chase – "Be the ball." That ancient wisdom can be applied to writing humor too.

In order to be the ball in humor you have to know the stuff humor is made of, you have to read as much humor as you can get your hands on from Moses to Captain Kirk. You then have to take what you've read and dissect it. Analyze what made it funny, to whom, and when. Was it really funny? Not so funny? Funny once, but not now? You have to get inside the humor until it becomes instinctive. That's right, you have to *be the humor*.

Let's take a looks at some old stuff. Here's an excerpt from an essay Mark Twain did called "Fennimore Cooper's Literary Offenses." I like this one because it's one writer ragging on another, even though the ragee was dead at the time. Still all of us in the writing profession need input from our peers from time to time. So in this essay, we not only have the biting, droll wit of one of America's greatest humorists, but also excellent tutelage in the skills of writing. I didn't include here all the writing violations Twain lists in the interest of space, but I would invite the reader to search out this essay and make it a part of his or her library.

Twain says this:

> There are nineteen rules governing literary art in the domain of romantic fiction—some say twenty-two. In Deerslayer Cooper violated eighteen of them. These require:

1. That a tale shall accomplish something and arrive somewhere. But the Deerslayer tale accomplishes nothing and arrives in the air...

The writing style is a little archaic, but that adds to its charm, and a lot of Mark Twain's writing is anything but PC by today's standard. Of course, in the late 19th Century and early 20th Century, people weren't so uptight about political correctness. Still, in the interest of more sensitivity, not to mention fewer lawsuits, I've edited out the more offensive things. But not so much that it detracts from Twain's brilliant humor… I hope.

3. They require that the personages in a tale shall be alive, except in the case of corpses, and that always the reader shall be able to tell the corpses from the others. But this detail has often been overlooked in the *Deerslayer* tale.

4. They require that the personages in a tale, both dead and alive, shall exhibit a sufficient excuse for being there. But this detail has also been overlooked in the *Deerslayer* tale.

5. They require that when the personages of a tale deal in conversation, the talk shall sound like human talk, and be talk such as human beings would be likely to talk in the given circumstances, and have a discoverable meaning, also a discoverable purpose, and a show of relevancy, and remain in the neighborhood of the subject in hand, and be interesting to the reader, and help out the tale, and stop when the people cannot think of anything more to say. But this requirement has been ignored from the beginning of the *Deerslayer* tale to the end of it...

7. They require that when a personage talks like an illustrated, gilt-edged, tree-calf, hand-tooled, seven-dollar Friendship's Offering in the

beginning of a paragraph, he shall not talk like a... minstrel in the end of it. But this rule is flung down and danced upon in the *Deerslayer* tale...

8. They require that crass stupidities shall not be played upon the reader as "the craft of the woodsman, the delicate art of the forest," by either the author or the people in the tale. But this rule is persistently violated in the *Deerslayer*...

I'm not exactly sure… no, I should say, I don't have the slightest idea what a "tree-calf" is or for that matter, the meaning of a "seven-dollar Friendship's Offering," but the point is well taken – a writer's character shouldn't change speaking style in mid-dialogue. And a writer should have some knowledge on a subject before he writes about it. Sound advice.

On the other hand, writing about a subject for which you have little or no first, or even second hand, knowledge; and writing in such a way that the reader will know you don't know, but meant to sound like you do know, and the reader knows that you know that he knows, can be very funny… you know?

Humorist Dave Barry is a master of this technique. I don't think James Fennimore Cooper used this technique, so Mark Twain's pointing it out makes Cooper look stupid and, therefore, funny.

Hey, you know and I know that, despite what our mothers said to us, making fun of some people can get us some laughs. That's why I thank God every day for giving us the French.

These remaining rules, except for 10, aren't necessarily hilarious, but I wanted to include them here because they're important rules for any writer.

> 10. They require that the author shall make the reader feel a deep interest in the personages... and in their fate; and that he shall make the reader love the good people in the tale and hate the bad ones. But the reader of the *Deerslayer* tale dislikes the good people in it, is indifferent to the others, and wishes they would all get drowned together.
>
> 11. They require that the characters in a tale shall be so clearly defined that the reader can tell beforehand what each will do in a given emergency...
>
> ...there are some little ones [rules]. These require that the author shall –
>
> 12. Say what he is proposing to say, not merely come near it.
>
> 13. Use the right word, not its second cousin.
>
> 14. Eschew surplusage [meaning avoid extra or non-existent words].
>
> 15. Not omit necessary details.
>
> 16. Avoid slovenliness of form.
>
> 17. Use good grammar.
>
> 18. Employ a simple straightforward style.

The next passage pretty much speaks for itself both on the writing critique and the humor content, but I wanted to include it because it's funny. The Cooper Indians were so funny, they would make the French cringe. In fact, if we could go back in time, I bet we'd find that the French allied with Cooper Indians against the British in the French &

Indian War and that's why they lost. With the French AND Cooper Indians, there's no way we (and the British) could have lost. Just a thought.

So read it and weep (with tears of laughter)…

Cooper's gift in the way of invention was not a rich endowment; but such as it was he liked to work it... In his little box of stage-properties he kept six or eight cunning devices... for his savages and woodsmen to deceive and circumvent each other with... A favorite one... that he pulled out... frequently was the broken twig. He prized the broken twig above all the rest of his effects, and worked it the hardest. It is a restful chapter in any book of his when somebody doesn't step on a dry twig and alarm all the reds and whites for two hundred yards around. Every time a Cooper person is in peril, and absolute silence is worth four dollars a minute, he is sure to step on a dry twig. There may be a hundred handier things to step on, but that wouldn't satisfy Cooper. Cooper requires him to... find a dry twig; and if he can't do it, go and borrow one...

...If Cooper had been an observer his inventive faculty would have worked better; not more interestingly, but more rationally, more plausibly... Cooper's eye was splendidly inaccurate. Cooper seldom saw anything correctly... In the *Deerslayer* Cooper has a stream which is fifty feet wide where it flows out of a lake; it presently narrows to twenty as it meanders along for no given reason, and yet when a stream acts like that it ought to be required to explain itself. Fourteen pages later the width of the brook's outlet from the lake has suddenly shrunk thirty feet, and becomes "the narrowest part of the stream." This shrinkage is not accounted for. The stream has bends in it, a sure indication that it has alluvial banks and cuts in them; yet these bends are only thirty and fifty feet long. If Cooper had been a nice... observer he would have noticed that the bends were oftener nine hundred feet long than short of it.

Cooper made the exit of that stream fifty feet wide, in the first place, for no particular reason; in the second place, he narrowed it to less than twenty to accommodate some Indians. He bends a "sapling" to the form of an arch over this narrow passage, and conceals six Indians in its foliage. They are "laying" for a settler's scow... which is coming up the stream on its way to the lake; it is being hauled against a stiff current by a rope whose stationary end is anchored in the lake; its rate of progress cannot be more than a mile an hour. Cooper describes the ark, but pretty obscurely. In the matter of dimensions "it was little more than a modern canal-boat." Let us guess, then, that it was about a hundred and forty feet long. It was of "greater breadth than common." Let us guess, then, that it was about sixteen feet wide. This leviathan had been prowling down bends which were but a third as long as itself, and scraping between banks where it had only two feet of space to spare on each side. We cannot too much admire this miracle. A low-roofed log dwelling occupies "two-thirds of the ark's length" – a dwelling ninety feet long and sixteen feet wide, let us say – a kind of vestibule train. The dwelling has two rooms – each forty-five feet long and sixteen feet wide, let us guess... The ark is arriving at the stream's exit now, whose width has been reduced to less than twenty feet to accommodate the Indians – say to eighteen [feet]. Did the Indians notice there was going to be a tight squeeze there? Did they notice that they could make money by climbing down out of that arched sapling and just stepping aboard when the ark scraped by? No, other Indians would have noticed these things, but Cooper's Indians never notice anything. Cooper thinks they are marvelous creatures for noticing, but he was almost always in error about his Indians. There was seldom a sane one among them.

The ark is one hundred and forty feet long; the dwelling is ninety feet long. The idea of the Indians is to drop softly and secretly from the arched sapling to the dwelling as the ark creeps along under it at the rate of a mile an hour, and butcher the family. It will take a minute and a half to pass under. It will take the ninety-foot dwelling a minute to pass under. Now, then, what did the six Indians do?... Their chief, a person of quite extraordinary intellect for a Cooper Indian, warily watched the canal-boat as it squeezed along under him, and when he had got his calculations fined down to exactly the right shade... he let go and dropped. And *missed the house!* That is exactly what he did. He missed the house, and landed in the stern of the scow. It was not much of a fall, yet it knocked him silly... If the house had been ninety-seven feet long he would have made the trip...

There still remained in the roost five Indians. The boat has passed under and is now out of their reach. Let me explain what the five did... No. 1 jumped for the boat, but fell in the water astern of it. Then No. 2 jumped for the boat, but fell in the water still farther astern of it. Then No. 3 jumped for the boat, and fell a good way astern of it. Then No. 4 jumped for the boat, and fell in

> the water *away* astern. Then No. 5 made a jump for the boat – for he was a Cooper Indian. In the matter of intellect, the differences between a Cooper Indian and the Indian that stands in front of the cigar-shop is not spacious...

Mark Twain said this: "Humor is only a fragrance, a decoration. Often it is merely an odd trick of speech and spelling."

It's important as a writer of humor to know what's funny and to read and hear what's funny. In most cases a sense of humor can be developed. I don't think you're born with the ability to be funny, although some people seem to have a certain bent in that direction. Like playing the piano all the practicing in the world won't get you to Carnegie Hall if you're tone deaf.

To keep going with this piano player metaphor, one can't become a piano virtuoso in a vacuum cleaner. To obtain keyboard virtuosity one must study the masters, by which I mean other piano players, not the golf tournament. And unless one has a photogenic memory, I'm willing to bet one has copies of masterpieces in one's piano bench written by the likes of Ludwig W. Beethoven, Wolfgang W. Mozart, Frederick W. Chopin, Elton W. John and Little W. Richard. For that very same reason, you, as the next humor writer genius need to…

Assemble a Looney Bin

Something that goes hand-in-hand with consuming humor with regularity is building a humor file. And the good news is, you don't need to have a piano bench to do it.

I have in the closet of my office at home an 18" X 18" x 18" cardboard storage box which my wife bought about fifteen years ago and covered with green paisley shelf paper. She originally got it to stick bank statements in, but I took it over as my looney bin. Since then, about fifteen years now, I've been cutting out newspaper columns, cartoons, magazine articles, whatever I find that strikes me funny or has the potential to have something funny written about it. I don't plagiarize other peoples work, you understand, but I may take something and work it from another angle, inject my own writing style and brand of humor.

My bin also serves as a good brain laxative when I get the so-called writer's block. Many times, after staring stupidly at the computer screen for hours trying to come up with, if not something semi-intelligent and interesting, at least something funny to write, I go to my little green paisley looney bin. Nothing like a stack of Dave Barry's, Dilberts, or Far Sides to get the old funny bone rattling again. There is a downside to this though. Sometimes their humor is so brilliant I get almost paralyzed with intimidation. I overcome this by picturing the author as William Shatner in his underwear. That's usually a sure cure, however, it can cause minor side effects, most commonly headache and nausea.

But here's another thought about being intimidated by the masters. I'll relate it in the form of an anecdote.

Back in my high school football playing days here in Oklahoma there was a team in our conference which was the perennial bully. Although to us they looked like Visigoths, they were called the Trojans. Yes, they were named after a condom. Year after year the Trojans were big and mean and tough and hairy and ugly and scary; and they usually won the conference championship. But conference champs or not, the Trojans beat us 56 to nothing every year. To say we were intimidated by them would be like saying Frenchmen don't often bathe. It would be grossly understated. We were so intimidated by them the very mention of their name caused us to whimper in our beds, much like a certain ex-president would at the thought of his senatorial wife catching him in an act of amorous dalliance.

In my sophomore year the superintendent of schools (it was a small town) came into our dressing room before the game with the Trojans and gave us a little speech. He was a fiery, bandy little guy who, it just so happened, had once been a Trojan. "Boys," he said. "You don't have anything to fear but fear itself. These guys aren't any different than you. They put their pants on one leg at a time. There's nothing they can do that you can't do just as well. If you let them intimidate you, the game's already lost. It's all up to you. Now what are we gonna do!" With that we went roaring out of the dressing room and onto the field eager to take on the Trojans.

That night they beat us 56 to nothing. But that speech by the superintendent stuck with me. When my senior year rolled around the Trojans only beat us 22-6.

My point is this: there will always be someone, or perhaps tens of someones, more talented, better connected, more socially adept, more politically adroit, luckier, richer, prettier, skinnier, taller than you. But the thing is you can't worry about them. That's an absolute waste of time and energy. What YOU've got to worry about are your own talents, and how you work to develop your skills, and raise the level of discipline in your work efforts, and enlarge your territory. You don't have to join the Army to be the best you can be. And nobody can bring you to your best except Old Number One.

NOW LET'S GET OUT THERE AND TAKE ON THE TROJANS OF THE WORLD, AND TRY TO KEEP THE SCORE CLOSE!!!

The World Outside the Looney Bin

Gathering humor can be fun… and intimidating. But there's a big wide world of sports out there from which much funny writing can be gleaned. Take for example:

Current Events

A friend of mine, Charles Sasser, is a prolific writer. He has written (and sold) about a billion books. Chuck is an adventurer, sort of a modern day Indiana Jones, who has spent most of his adult life living on the edge. He was in the Navy, the Green Berets, spent at least two tours in Viet Nam, that I'm aware of, was a Miami and Tulsa cop, has flown an ultra-lite powered parachute across the country (a record), took up kick boxing at age 55, and for all I know, personally dropped a bunker buster on at least one of Saddam Hussein's palaces. I had written Chuck an e-mail a few weeks back and finally got a reply – "Sorry I didn't answer sooner, Phil," he replied. "I just got back from Algiers." *Algiers*, for crying out loud! I wrote him back, "Not a prob, Chuck. I just got back from Wal-Mart."

Well, what I wanted to tell you about Chuck is that he got this idea to write a book about the stupid things liberals do. He started scouring the newspaper for items demonstrating that, filled a bucket with clippings, wrote up a book, sold it, and is now on the conservative talk radio circuit talking to hosts and listeners about what he wrote. A gold mine on his doorstep, with just a little perception and cleverness on his part.

Maybe you could write a book on the stupid things conservatives do, or stupid things moderates do, or stupid things Islamic extremists do, or stupid things Methodists do. I'm sure they've all got equal time in that department. None of us, no matter what socio-economic group we fall into, are immune to stupidity. That's because human stupidity is pandemic and always has been since Eve ate the apple. It's also subjective. No one is stupid, or does anything stupid until someone else points it out.

The thing is, with a little head scratching and open eyes and ears to which way the wind is blowing, you could find subject matter that would appeal to some group of readers. Try to find the humor in it and exploit that. Not everybody may think it's funny, but chances are some will. The trick here is to pick a group or issue that a lot of people would like to see made fun of. However, in this day and age of political correctness and social sensitivity, you should be either insightful enough to not be offensive, or strong enough to withstand the backlash. That's why I pick on the French. They're Caucasian, European, and generally unlikable. Who could possibly be offended. The French, you say? So what. They don't like anybody anyway, and are taught from birth to be snotty.

Personal experiences

Take it from me, if there's one thing you're more knowledgeable about than anyone else, it's your own personal experiences. This can be a treasure trove of humor writing. In fact, if you're going to write about your personal experiences, my advice is to inject them with a lot of humor. The fact is, unless you're like my friend Chuck Sasser and are constantly off battling Nazis and your occasional totalitarian regime for archeological treasures, chances are nobody is likely to be that interested in reading about what you've done. Not editors, anyway; and that's where it starts. That's not to say you may have experienced something inspirational, uplifting, or economically successful. Magazines like Guideposts and Reader's Digest are full of those kinds of stories. If that's the case with you, by all means, write it up and sell it to them. But this is a book about humor writing, and nobody cares about your trip to Wal-Mart unless you've got something funny to say about it.

One of the best techniques for writing funny Wal-Mart personal experience stories is the use of self-deprecation. Self-deprecation, for those of you living due south of Brighton, England, comes from the Greek *selfos*, meaning "funny" and the Latin *deprecari*, meaning "trips to Wal-Mart." And much like Wal-Mart, that leads to a tendency to undervalue oneself and one's abilities.

Self-deprecating humor has two advantages – 1. It endears you to the reader because he or she can identify with your shortcomings. 2. By disparaging yourself and your own abilities, it makes your readers at the same time feel superior and empathetic. Self-deprecation sells.

Let's do an exercise. Here's a commonplace personal experience written in first person dull:

A Trip to Wal-Mart

One evening, I needed some AAA batteries for my son, so I went to Wal-Mart to get some. While I was there, I picked up some things for my wife. The Wal-Mart store in our town is very big, but the people who work there are nice. HA, HA.

Now you might be like me and say to yourself, after comparing yourself to someone like Chuck Sasser, "Nothing exciting ever happens to me. I live a very ordinary, boring life." That may be absolutely true, but that doesn't mean your writing needs to be.

Okay, let's take that very same excruciatingly dull "personal experience" and see if we can't come up with something a little more interesting and appealing to read, humor being our main ingredient, of course:

Why Do We Go to Wal-Mart? Because it's There.

All I needed was some triple A batteries for our walkie-talkies.

See, my son lives mostly upstairs with his door closed, and after years of shouting and knocking on the walls to get him to come to supper, we decided maybe it would be a good idea to invest in a couple of cheap, wireless, communication devices. These work very well for the most part, and my wife and I take turns kicking each other whenever the subject comes up for not doing it years before. (Just between you and me, I try not to talk about it anymore, but there's not a day goes by she doesn't bring it up. I think she just uses it as an excuse to kick me.)

I say these gizmos work well "for the most part" because of their being open channel wireless thingies. We generally get through to our son with them, but we also pick up your occasional skateboarders cruising through the neighborhood. Have you ever heard these guys talk?

"Say, doo, ah sippin da ray fo ma mickin forcep dow da freezin. Yo?" [*screech*]

"Nah, lez trazon fo eggis nahmin. Aw ite?" [*screech*]

"Aw ite." [*screech*]

During the next big war, if the government runs out of Navajos to transmit coded messages, they should draft these guys.

We have to time it so that we don't call Nate to supper when the skateboarders are around, otherwise it confuses all of us. And, no, a different channel won't work. They eventually track us down.

So, anyway, all I needed was some batteries, right? "I'm going to get some batteries," I said to my wife.

"Where are you going?" she asked. *Uh-oh*, I thought to myself

"To get some batteries," I said.

"What STORE, I mean," she said.

"A store with batteries," I said. *Please, God, no!*

"Why don't you go to Wal-Mart? I need some things."

She hastily wrote out a list and handed it to me. I said nothing. I just took the list and went out to the garage and got in the car. Then, while sitting there in the darkness, I put my head on the steering wheel and wept bitterly.

It's not that I don't think Wal-Mart is a fine company, or that they don't have fine stores with wonderfully abundant, well-priced merchandise. It's not that I don't think their employees are friendly and helpful and strangely cheerful. It's not that I don't know that without Wal-Mart in our economy America would become Uganda or France. It just that their stores and parking lots are so... so... vast. In the future, when scientists talk of the distances between the planets in our Solar System, they will replace Astronomical Units with Wal-Mart Units to make the expanses more understandable – Distance from the sun to Pluto = 4,000,000,000 miles or 2 W.U.

No matter what time of day you go to a Wal-Mart the only parking slot available is the one located next to the street. Even then you have to get out of the car and push the five or so empty shopping carts out of it before you can pull in. The store from there is just a glow on the horizon, if it's night. If it's daylight, it's best to have some Boy Scout skills, or at least a Boy Scout with you, to find an entrance. I was lucky this day. A cart guy came in the nick of time, waved cheerfully to me, hurriedly gathered up the carts, and motioned me into the parking place. I zipped into the slot and quickly jumped out to follow him to the store before he disappeared in the distance.

When I finally walked into the front entrance, I smiled at the older gentleman standing inside. I nodded to him and said, "How're you doing today."

"Whatzat?" he replied.

"HOW ARE YOU DOING TODAY?" I repeated.

"Yeah, it sure is," he said. "You need a cart?"

"No thanks. I'm fine."

"What?"

I smiled again and shook my head no. If I was going to gather up all the things my wife had on that list, I sure as heck would need a cart, but my pride wouldn't permit me to take one. Real men didn't push shopping carts through Wal-Mart.

As I walked past the "foyer" and into the front of the store, it opened up before me like a cosmic dome. You'd get claustrophobic in Carlsbad Caverns next to this store. I must have been standing there with my mouth open, because a very friendly young man with blond hair and a blue vest approached me and said, "Can I help you find something, sir?"

"Yeah," I said still looking into the distant haze near the other end of the store. After a few seconds, I looked at him. I could see enthusiasm in his eyes and a bright friendly happy expression on his face. You could tell he was eager to please me. If he'd started panting, it would've been hard to distinguish him from a golden retriever.

I looked forlornly down at my wife's list. "Where would I find the... um... well... feminine products?"

He didn't hesitate. I obviously wasn't his first husband shopper. "Go down this main aisle to double P, turn left and follow that through Housewares until you get to Business Supplies. From there veer to the right until you see a sign that says 'Phoenix, 2 miles.' You're almost there. Keeping the lawn tractors on your right and after about 100 yards, turn left at the next

> intersection, then right, then right again, then left.
>
> A couple of hours later, laden with a dozen bulging blue plastic bags, I walked past a different older gentleman at the entrance. There must have been an older gentleman shift change since I came in.
>
> "Thanks for shopping at Wal-Mart," he said.
>
> I grinned and hefted my bags. "Quite a load," I said to him.
>
> "Whatzat?" he said.
>
> When I got home, the wife helped me un-bluebag everything and put it away. A nice gesture. But she looked puzzled.
>
> "So," she asked. "Where are your batteries?"
>
> It was a rhetorical question.

Okay. A little more interesting than the first version, huh? Hopefully, a little funnier too. Did you notice the use of self-deprecation? Unless you have an ego the size of Bill O'Reilly's, self-deprecation isn't hard to do. And I couldn't have gotten into the heart of the story if I hadn't led into it with a little humor about…

Marriage

Nothing can be more humorous, or tragic, than married life. Take my wife, please. No, I'm just kidding. With the possible exception of airline travel, nothing has been written and laughed about more than marriage. That's because nothing is funnier than a man and woman of the opposite sex legally living together and sharing expenses.

The possibilities are endless for humorous material on this topic, that is, if you approach it this way. I know people, even friends, who have gone through very bitter divorces and can't, or won't, find anything funny about living one single day with that other person. Perhaps if they'd searched out a little humor, there wouldn't have been so much bitterness in the end and afterward.

Oh well, I'm certainly no marriage counselor, but I have managed to stay married to the same woman for thirty years at this writing. And she never once thought about divorce… murder, yes, but not divorce (an old joke, I know, but truth makes it funny).

Staying married this long is probably more a testament to my wife than me. Thirty years from my side has been pretty darn easy and pleasant. Not so sure about her side of the story. That's not to say we haven't had a fight or two. But who hasn't?

The main thing is, we keep it light. There's not a day goes by, and hasn't gone by, that we don't laugh together or find something about ourselves and our relationship that we think is funny.

Here's one example:

Why I'm Not as Stupid as I Look

"The smartest thing you ever did was marry Darlene."

I've been told that by numerous people over the years - my mother, my father, my mother-in-law, my tax man, the Schwan's man, my vet, my lawyer, my mechanic, my probation officer... the list goes on and on. But to tell you the truth, twenty-nine years ago I didn't appear all that smart.

As a typical example, in the spring of 1973 I was moonlighting nights and weekends at a wallpaper wholesaler to supplement my $500 dollar a month teacher's pay in Dallas, Texas. One Sunday afternoon, before we were married, I took Darlene and $50 cash over to some guy's house and bought his last wiener dog puppy. This wasn't smart for two reasons: 1 - a $50 wiener dog was not in my meager budget; 2 - any fool knows you shouldn't buy the last of anything, especially the last of a litter, especially the last of a litter of wiener dogs. This would prove itself true many times over the next several years.

And I don't think I scored very high on her folks Potential Son-In-Law IQ Test, either. The first time she took me home to meet the family we sat down to a nice Sunday dinner served on her mother's finest china set on an heirloom lace tablecloth.

I won't say I was nervous, but I did manage to turn over my goblet of iced tea about halfway through the meal.

"Holy cow," I stammered, mopping up the spilled tea with my linen napkin. "I hope this tablecloth wasn't expensive."

"This tablecloth," my future mother-in-law said graciously trying to hide her irritation. "Came from Sweden, and has been in my family for three generations."

"Oh, thank goodness," I said with a sigh of relief. "I'm glad it wasn't new.

Despite my obvious stupidity, Darlene married me and we took off on our so far twenty-nine year journey. And as it turns out, all those people were right, about my marrying her being the smartest thing I ever did. And I've been thinking about all the reasons it was a smart move:

- I found a friend.

- I found a friend who has stayed my friend even when I'm stupid.

-She brought me to life-long friends I may otherwise have missed.

- She loves my family and my family loves her.

-She brought me into a her family who made me a part of them (after a 4-1 vote).

- She blessed me with two magnificent children.

- She made me feel important.

- She showed me the light of God through her shining spirit.

And what did she get out of the deal? She got to move around a lot. Suffer through the ups and downs of job changes. Experience all the thick and thin, then back to thick. And, of course, there was that $50 wiener dog.

I once heard a man say, "If it wasn't for sex, men and women would have killed each other off long ago." Which brings us to our next topic for finding humorous writing material…

Children

Right next to marriage and airline travel for the biggest source of humor writing material is children, especially for those of us who have some. Almost every modern-day humorist has written extensively about their children, and who wouldn't. The little darlings cause more heartburn, panic, anxiety, anger, fear, grief, and aggravation than anything else in the world.

As the great American humorist and father Bill Cosby said to one of his TV children, "I brought you into the world, and I can take you out." I have no doubt he probably originally said that to all of his real children. The thing, though, that keeps me personally from following through with such a threat is my pure unadulterated, polyunsaturated unconditional love for them. I've said, I really never knew what love was until I had a child.

When I was a young father in my early thirties - my son being about a year old at the time - I got to thinking about all the stupid, snotty things I did as a kid and teenager. I was sitting with my dad (the greatest man I've ever known) on the porch, as my son threw one of his one-year-old ring-tailed tooter fits. Right then and there I apologized to Pop for being such really rotten, stinking kid. He just chuckled and said, "That's okay, son, I get great comfort in knowing you're getting yours."

I guess all the crap we have to put up with as a parent just comes with the territory, and then our kids get there turn. As the cliché says, what goes around comes around.

In the meantime, there's no reason we can't try to make a little money by writing about our rotten little rug monkeys. Actually, I've found out you never run out of material when it comes to your kids. My youngest is twenty-two. I started writing stuff about her the day she was born. I wrote this column about her only six months ago:

One Person's Stupid is Another's Nose Screw

This edition comes under the heading, "Factors That Contribute to the Alarming Increase in Paternal Insanity."

My daughter, who is now twenty-one, moved into her "own place" this summer with two other girls. They took up residence in a small rental house in the town, about an hour's drive from here, where she attends college.

Now that she's not officially a part of our household, I look forward to seeing her on occasional visits. And this time it was really good to see most of her; however, the one part of her I wasn't real thrilled about seeing was her nose. That's because her nose had a small sparkly blue stone stuck into one side of it.

I must have looked less than ecstatic when I first saw it, because she said, "What's the matter, daddy, don't you like it?"

The question was a no-brainer for a fifty-seven year old white male, who also happened to be the inquisitor's dad.

"No," came my unequivocal answer.

"Why not?" she continued, giving me the impish dimpled smile I'd come to know only too well these past two decades.

"Because it looks stupid," I said. "What possible reason could you have for wanting to stick something like that into your beautiful face?"

"I've just been wanting to do this for awhile, and I finally got up the nerve and Scott wanted me to get a tattoo with him, but I said, 'no way, those are dumb,' and he wanted me to go with him anyway so I said okay and while I was there I decided to go ahead and get this nose screw."

"You didn't answer my question," I said.

"What question?"

"Why would you do such a thing?"

"I just told you."

"That wasn't an explanation, that was blather."

"Oh, Dad, I don't see what the big deal is. Lot's of people my age do this. Besides, it's very small and cute.

She had a point. At least it wasn't a big stainless steel bolt through her nose, or through her tongue, or through God knows where else... so far, anyway. And she did come out against tattoos... at least, I think she did. Still, we are a mature, conservative dad and we can't abide this kind of foolishness from our young.

"The big deal is," I said. "This time next year you're going to be a college graduate out looking for a job, and guys like me, or a female equivalent, are going to be interviewing you. They're going to take one look at that spike in your nose, and no matter how cool or cute it may appear to you and your colleagues, they're going to mentally note, *flake, undependable, immature, rebellious*, and whatever other negative perception that thing gives them. Maybe none of that is true, but that's the impression it will leave, and regardless of your abilities, skills, and credentials, you will not, in all likelihood, make their short list."

"Whatever," she replied, giving me the standard eye roll she has reserved for just such lectures for the past eight years.

That's pretty much where we left it. On Sunday of that weekend, we attended church together, had a nice dinner, and she packed up to head back to her new home. Nothing else was said about the nose pin or stud or screw or whatever the heck it is. I tried to ignore it, and she didn't bring it up. Standing by her car, we hugged and I kissed her forehead and told her to be careful going back and she said she would, just like any other weekend before she went back to school.

As I waved goodbye from the driveway and then turned to head back inside, I was suddenly glad she hadn't asked me about some of the stupid things I'd done as a twenty-one year old.

And then all this love and marriage and accompanying children can be bundled up into one big happy pile of humor material called…

Home Life

This topic can cover a lot of ground, especially if you have a big yard. But seriously, folks, home life can be rife with humor material if yours is anything like mine, which is anything like most Americans (sorry, I can't speak for the French home life which probably involves French-speaking people and very little soap.)

The best example of humorous home life writing probably came from the late Erma Bombeck. When I was a teenager, my mom would sit down every Tuesday morning with a cup of coffee and the newspaper and laugh out loud as she read Erma's column.

When Mom finished, she'd shake her head and wipe away tears and say, "That Erma Bombeck hits the nail right on the head." Erma Bombeck was to moms and wives as Dave Barry is to guys. But she had a universal appeal because she could make us all relate to the tumbled, helter skelter, imperfect, hilarious and many times poignant environment of our home life.

You would do well to study Mrs. Bombeck's writing, not just for the examples of home life material, but for humor writing in general. She is one of the icons of American humor. Unfortunately, the Bombeck family wouldn't give me permission to reprint one of her columns here as an example, but don't let that stop you. Examples of her writing are not hard to find. Several books of her compiled columns are still on the market. Whole cottage industries, if not cults, pertaining to Erma Bombeck exist. Just type "Bombeck" into your favorite search engine on the 'Net, and you'll find page after page of references.

What makes Bombeck's personal story appealing to us writers is the fact that she wrote about her every day life in her hometown newspaper, got picked up by a syndicate, and lived the writer's dream we all dream. So if we go to school on her, maybe we can realize the dream too.

Speaking of school, there's plenty of humor to be found in…

Academia

Most of us have spent a ton of time in and around schools for a big portion of our lives. For those of us who have children that time multiplies what with PTA's, meeting with teachers and counselors, meeting with principals and law enforcement officers, school plays, school carnivals, school sporting events. But the funny stuff doesn't stop there. When your kids move on to college, as mine have, that opens up a whole new galaxy of potential humor writing.

So whether you're a student, a former student, a parent of a student, a teacher (bless you) you've no doubt got a super tanker load of material from which to draw.

One of the funniest examples of humor from academia comes from Professor Anders Henriksson's (Shepherd College, West Virginia) compilation of some of his students' mangled interpretation of history, logic, spelling, and grammar over the years. He points out that, although hilarious, these "out-takes" come from his many years in the teaching business, and are by no means representative of an entire generation of scholars.

The book is entitled *Non Campus Mentis* (Workman Publishing Company, New York, NY), and if it's not part of your library, you should immediately make it so. I will guarantee you side-splitting, air-gasping laughter when you read it. And then again, as many times as you re-read it.

For some strange reason known only to them, (I'm guessing it involves lawyers) the Workman people wouldn't allow me to reprint anything from Professor Henriksson's book, but trust me, the book is full of hilarity. So I did something I think I do very well. After a first failed attempt, I wrote them back an I begged them. "Surely," I wrote, "the plug for your book would be worth just one little example, and surely you wouldn't mind that." But they answered, "We said *no* and we mean *NO*, and quit calling us Shirley."

It's not nearly as funny as what I wanted to put here from *Non Campus Mentis*, but here's a piece I wrote about some of my school years. Oh, and I changed my mind. Don't go buy *Non Campus Mentis*. You will only end up in the emergency room with severely split sides which will cost you way more than the price of the book.

Second Grade – It Takes a Little Luck

Luck hasn't always been my lady, but a time existed in the second grade when she did agree to go out with me. Believe me, it couldn't have come at a better time. I was flunking arithmetic, and had just gotten paddled for punching Pudge Hargrove in the stomach. You see, Pudge had demanded my chair in reading circle and attempted to sit on me when I refused. As much as she out-weighed me a good twenty pounds, I pleaded self-defense. But Mrs. Walker, being of the old school where boys didn't hit girls under any circumstances, overruled.

My troubles all started when my oldest sister Pat planned on having her first child in a place called San Antonio, and my mother, a rookie grandmother, had decided to attend the birthing. That would've been fine, except she left my sister Michele and me with Daddy. That would've been fine too, except Daddy had butchered a hog in the fall, and decided to put us on an all-pork diet until Mom got back. One week during that time I got the flu, so Aunt Velma, Daddy's sister, came up from Tulsa to stay with us, and tried to feed me milk toast. Uncle Erwin, she said, loved milk toast when he had an upset stomach. When I told Daddy about it that evening, he said that Uncle Erwin was a pansy, if you wanted his opinion.

So between Daddy's salted pig, Aunt Velma's food for the gastronomically limited, and my scholastic difficulties, Michele and I were on the verge of setting off in search of Mom. Finding San Antonio, we reasoned, could be no worse than more days of salty ham and soft poached eggs on rye.

The next Monday at school Mrs. Walker would pass out report cards. The principal's call to conference with Daddy regarding the Pudge Hargrove Incident hadn't set well with him, and now, if I brought home a "U" (Unsatisfactory) in arithmetic, well... That's when Lady Luck accepted my collect call.

"Philip, I want to speak to you after class," Mrs. Walker said. She wore her hair in a bun twisted on top of her head which she used as a pencil holder. She had two sharp ones usually stuck into it. Her thick glasses magnified her small eyes, and she pursed her lips making her look like a dried apricot with headlights. She wasn't a bad woman though, merely intense about the business of instructing seven-year-olds.

Earlier, she had said, "Philip, go to the board and complete problem three." Mrs. Walker believed in the Board Problem Method of teaching public humiliation, and used it extensively.

Gulping back dread as thick as cold molasses, I walked to the front of the room with chains around my legs. Sniggers bombarded me from every direction. By February of that year, my reputation at the board had become legend. As I passed George Botts, he bit his tongue and slapped the top of his desk to suppress his mirth.

At the board I stared at the chalk horror in front of me.

"Read us the problem, please," Mrs. Walker said from the pulpit of her desk.

"Nine hundred thousand, fifty..."

More titters.

"Nine *thousand*, nine hundred fifty," she corrected.

"Nine thousand, nine hundred fifty and two..."

"Holy cow," George Botts snorted. The class howled.

"Class," Mrs. Walker warned, and snapped her fingers twice. Silence returned, but facing the board I could still hear the grins. My face burned as if bared to an August sun.

"...take away fifty hund...

"*Fie-ev* hundred," she said.

"...five hundred f-f-for...I mean, fifty-seven."

"Very good. Now figure the answer."

In the second grade, any correct answers I got to arithmetic problems came by divine messenger, and not by reason. I hastily wrote an eight, a four, and two fives beneath the problem's horizontal chalk line. It was wrong, of course. Mercifully, Mrs. Walker let me return to my seat, judiciously ignoring the left jab I sent to a gasping George Botts' shoulder as he tried not to fall out of his seat in his hysteria.

"Philip," Mrs. Walker said once we were alone that afternoon. "I wanted to talk to you about your arithmetic grade." I started mentally working out my plans for the road trip to San

Antonio. "I know your mother has been gone for several weeks, and with your father taking care of you, you're probably not eating right, and..."

A ray of sunshine cut through my gloom. "Yes ma'am," I blurted. "It's the ham. And Aunt Velma's been trying to make us eat pansy food, and..."

"What?" She looked confused at my outburst, and somewhat perturbed that I had interrupted her. Her brow furrowed. Her lips pursed. Her eyes flashed to high beam. I buttoned my lip.

"Well, anyway, I know your mother would be upset if you brought home this 'U' in arithmetic, so I'm going to change it to an 'I' (Incomplete) if you promise me you will study very hard this last nine weeks."

"Oh, yes ma'am," I said.

So Lady Luck paid me a visit in the second grade. I was darn lucky my mom had taken off for southern Texas, so that my teacher felt sorry for me, thinking me semi-orphaned, and flunking arithmetic because of excessive wimp food and a pork overdose.

As it turned out, I was flunking arithmetic because I couldn't see the blackboard and needed glasses. The nature of my problem finally dawned on Mrs. Walker during one of her stints as playground warden. She watched as George Botts threw me a softball which I missed with my hands, but stopped with my forehead...three times.

And, of course, the whole reason for school is to find a career, and/or your children to find a career. Or, more importantly, a job. Once we do step into that wonderful enchanting world of work, there is no end to the material at hand for writing humor.

Careers/Jobs

You all recall the famous proletarian words of that famous American proletariat Tina Turner (written by John Fogerty) when she said:

"Left a good job in the city,
Workin' for The Man ev'ry night and day,
And I never lost one minute of sleepin',
Worryin' 'bout the way things might have been.
Big wheel keeps on turnin'
Proud Mary keeps on churnin'
Rollin', rollin, rollin down the river."

And then the follow-up comments by her back-up group:

"WHOOP! Whoop, whoop, whoop.
WHOOP! Whoop, whoop, whoop."

I couldn't have said it better even if I'd been Ike (Turner, for those of you in generations later than Boomer). In fact, now that I've shed the surly bonds of corporate life, this is now one of my personal theme songs (I have several, depending on the situation). When they do a sitcom based on my life, this will be my lead-in music. In my working lifetime, I've probably had well over five jobs, some I've left of my own volition, some have left me of their own volition. ("Phil, your size no longer fits our needs, so, like an old horse, we're putting you down. Get it? Downsized? Heh, heh. Just a little lay-off humor. Well, anyway, we appreciate all your 10-12 hour days at no extra pay, your not griping too much about your 3% annual raises, and for clapping when the CEO came around to make company-wide speeches. This security guard will escort you out.

Bruno, I don't think the cuffs will be necessary. So, thanks a million, and don't let the door hit you in the butt on the way out. Heh, heh.") All, in some form or fashion had their funny moments. And I'm sure you can say the same thing. Who hasn't experienced the micro-management of an uptight boss, or the stumbling incompetence of fellow and fellowette cube-mates, or the tyrannical repression of those IT goons. Well, here's an example I wrote a couple years back… before my last two lay-offs:

> This week's topic on Why Not Ask Phil deals with concerns about the work place. We will answer questions not so much of a highly technical nature concerning some of those computer thingies, but rather more on the geeks who run them.
>
> Q: What is it with these people who operate the office computer network?
>
> A: Every company I've ever been associated with has a close knit group of these people whom all the other employees refer to as The Network Nazis. It's the Network Nazis' job to run the company's computer network like a 1939 German railroad while being as disagreeable and difficult to deal with as is humanly possible without everyone taking up a collection to have them stuffed into the nearest file server.
>
> Q: Well, what makes these Network Nazis so disagreeable?
>
> A: For one thing, 1939 German railroads didn't "go down" intermittently and for no apparent reason. But aside from that, the number of network infractions your average user can commit would fill volumes. In fact, they do and are listed alphabetically in all those thick

volumes you see stacked side by side on the shelves above the desk of the main Network Nazi – The Netvurkenfuhrer - and labeled "Netvurken Administratahoben." However, the Network Nazis' main hot buttons are users' excessive use of disk space, which includes but is not limited to: sending and re-sending e-mail with attached animated pictures of babies and/or puppies/kitties as well as forwarding copies of "The Top 1000 Reasons Men Are Stoopider Than Womens" to no fewer than 100 co-workers, and unauthorized installation of the multi-user space combat game Dork Wars.

Q: What about them Help Desk personnel?

A: These are a variation on your Network Nazi, only less powerful. Some may be Network Nazi trainees; while others may be serial killers. The most important quality to being a good Help Desk Person is attitude. A Help Desk Person can never have too much attitude. Saying a Help Desk Person has too much attitude would be like saying Al Gore has too much charisma, or Wal-Mart has too many stores, or the president and Congress are giving us too many tax cuts, or I make too much money, and so on. Generally speaking, you know a Help Desk Person is in a good mood when a phone conversation with them goes something like this:

HDP: (sigh) Helpdeskwhaddayaneed?

YOU: Yes, um, I got this message on my screen that says "The program you're running has caused an inexcusable error, and I dang sure don't like it. If this problem persists, call Microsoft to prevent further hair loss." What should I do?

HDP: Re-boot.

YOU: Is that it?

HDP: That's the short version.

YOU: What's the long version?

HDP: You're an idiot. Shut-up and re-boot, stupid.

And that's usually from a Help Desk Person who's in their first day on the job. I've seen really experienced and skilled Help Desk Persons make grown men, even ex-Marines with visible tattoos, whimper for their mothers. The good news is, you don't have to deal with these folks for more than about a week as they tend to mutate attitude-wise into the big version of Sigourney Weaver's space alien and move on to greener pastures; the two best examples of this being Dr. Laura and Hillary Clinton. But the bad news is, there always seems to be another one to take its place.

Q: How do you explain those weirdoes called programmers?

A: These creatures are very hard to explain, because they are not, as a rule, from this planet. No wait, let me re-phrase that. They are not from this dimension, by which I mean a place where humans interact socially without once bringing up the mandelbrot vs. julia set of fractals and/or Star Trek. Some scientists believe that modern day programmers (Nerdus Billgatesi) evolved from dinosaurs known as Geekopods and Fortranabanana fauna who roamed the earth during the Vacuumtubocene Era over 50 years ago. Of course, those scientists who believe that, like programmers, never had prom dates either, so you have to make allowances when considering their opinions.

Q: Do any of these people make our jobs easier?

A: It's not a question of them making our jobs easier. It's a question of why have these people develop such atypical eating habits, dress, hygiene, hair, and head piercings. Furthermore, in today's fast-paced, high-tech business world, no job is ever meant to be fulfilling, meaningful, and rewarding. Jobs of the '00's are designed to help make as much money as possible for the owner or owners before the persons doing the work actually go slobber slinging crazy. That's why such famous schools of business such as Harvard, Yale, and Bob's Big School of Bidness put such a strong emphasis on future CEO's learning the concept of downsizing. So all of us, in today's ever-changing work environment, should not look on our fellow workers with derision and contempt. Instead, we should strive to work harmoniously and relatively gun-free with all types of oddballs we meet in the workplace regardless of race, creed, or ethnic background.

Of course, all work and no play makes Phil a dull boy, so they say. And humor material also abounds in…

Sports

You don't necessarily have to participate in sports to write something funny about them. For instance, if you're a wife or girl friend with no interest in athletics, no doubt you have a lot of derogatory (and humorous) things to say about your significant other's sports involvement. On the other hand, if you're basically a guy couch potato like me, there's lots of fun to make on women vs. sports. Take, for example, what Dave Barry once said :

"If a woman has to choose between catching a fly ball and saving an infant's life, she will choose to save the infant's life without even considering if there is a man on base."

Sports figures themselves can be a source of great funniness. Here's some quotes from some athletes I got in one of those multi-forwarded e-mails:

A senior basketball player at the University of Pittsburgh said: "I'm going to graduate on time, no matter how long it takes."

Football commentator and former player Joe Theismann: "Nobody in football should be called a genius. A genius is a guy like Norman Einstein."

Stu Grimson, Chicago Blackhawks left wing, explaining why he keeps a color photo of himself above his locker: "That's so when I forget how to spell my name, I can still find my clothes."

Shaquille O'Neal, on whether he had visited the Parthenon during his visit to Greece: "I can't really remember the names of all the clubs we went to."

Frank Layden, Utah Jazz president, on a former player: "I told him, 'Son, what is it with you? Is it ignorance or apathy? He said,'Coach, I don't know and I don't care.'"

We've discussed a half a dozen or so places where you can find humor and write about it, but the list is nearly infinite, limited only by your imagination and sense of humor.

Take a moment to sit down and brain storm. Get a pencil and pad, or just open a blank sheet on your favorite word processor, and write down whatever pops into your mind in the way of humor topics. You'll be surprised how quickly that list grows. Just about anything will fit. In addition to what we've already touched on, here are a few more items bulging with funny things for you to write about:

Unforgettable Characters

All of us have people in our lives who are odd or eccentric or just plain funny. Maybe you know someone who is all of the above. So much the better. Write about them. There are several markets interested in these kinds of stories. But remember the Golden Rule here. We don't want to be cruel to real individuals for a couple of reasons. 1 – It could come back to bite you, especially if it's libelous. 2 – Writing with a mean spirit is pretty transparent. Unless your readers are Third World despots or terrorists or French, most people will see through your unkindness and not consider it funny.

Consumer goods and services

Who of us, in this abundant, free enterprise society hasn't experienced a laugh or two in this arena. Think of a time (or times) you paid for something that didn't turn out quite as advertised. Now take that frustration (and miffedness) and put a humorous spin to it. Most fellow consumers can relate. Want a really good source for humor material in this category? Pick up any assembly/-installation/user's guide for any household appliance. Mountains of humor material there. Pay particular attention to the warnings section, e.g., "WARNING! Do not use this product (hair dryer) while showering." Not only will you get volumes of material, you will get it in at least three languages. I especially like the ones translated from an

Asian language to English – “The electrical is to not plugging in wetness.”

Travel

The travel writing market always seems to be looking for a few good writers, especially those who write with wit.

Church or religion

You’d be surprised how many religious or church periodicals or newsletters want humor. material

Hobby

Not only can you make money writing about your hobby, but if you can inject some humor, you’re even more likely to sell it.

Relatives/In-laws

Don’t need to elaborate on this. We all have funny relatives or in-laws on which we could write volumes.

Pets

I probably don’t need to tell you that folks are weird about their pets, especially dogs and cats. Heck, I’m no exception. But the thing is, people who love their pets love to read about other peoples pets.

The list of topics for humor writing could go on and on, limited only by your imagination. What I’ve put down here is only a sampling out of my own limited mind.

If You're Nuts, You'll Need Bolts

Caution, Humor Writer Zone

Wanting to write humor is one thing; having the means, mechanics, and skills to do it is quite another. It's not totally mandatory, but you should have a few basic things to set up shop as any kind of a writer, humor or otherwise.

Dude, you should get a Dell

I know idealists in our profession will tell you having a computer and printer and the latest word-processing software won't make you a writer, and they will be absolutely right. On the other hand, they sure wouldn't hurt.

I once heard from a professor that Thomas Wolfe (the *Look Homeward Angel* one, not the *The Right Stuff* one) used to write in longhand standing up with a legal pad and pencil. That could be true or it could be an urban legend? Either way, what's totally amazing is that I was awake long enough in one of my college literature classes to remember that, and that it stuck with me all these years. Still, urban legend or not, here in the Twenty-First Century, writing longhand in any position would be down-right igernant.

I also heard from a master carpenter that you can't be a master anything if you don't have the right tools for the job. Tools won't make you a master carpenter or master mechanic or master wordsmith, but not having them will make your getting to that level a whole lot harder and take you a whole lot longer. Conceivably, it could prevent your attaining that level altogether.

You X and Y genners (I'm a Boomer) probably can't remember anything before electronic keyboards and computer monitors, but back in my day [pause to spit towards the flower bed and scratch my grizzled old gray beard] I had to stand up to write my first novel in longhand with a pencil and pad.

Why I remember in the Winter of '69 I had to type my senior paper on a contraption known as a Smith-Corona typewriter. Didn't have one of them delete keys neither. No, sir. You made a mistake, you erased it by hand, backed up, and typed her agin; either that, or start plum over. And if you wanted a copy, you put what 'uz knowed as carbon paper between your main copy and a second sheet. It was a long, laborious process, unless you could afford to pay some industrious co-ed with typing skills better'n yorn fifty cents a page to do it for ya. That's usually what I done. Then I could use my time more productively by going down to the local pub and networking.

So what I'm saying is spend the money to get the right writing tools and spend your time writing, not wasting it with poor tools. You can expend about five hundred dollars and get the bare minimum of a computer, printer, and word-processing program, and still be light-years ahead of where I was in 1969. Spend about a thousand more and you can have state of the art including broadband Internet access.

But what am I talking about. A lot of you probably got laptops as baby gifts.

While the places to submit stuff electronically is growing daily, there are still many places where you must submit your stuff the old fashioned way – a printed hardcopy in an envelope, sent by snail mail, with the obligatory SASE enclosed (Self-Addressed Stamped Envelope for those of you living east of the English Channel). The reason I'm bringing all this up is to discuss a printer. You need a good quality printer – laser or inkjet. The good news is you can buy a very good one of these for a lot less than you could even five years ago. I've got a good laser printer I bought (about 5 years ago) for about $600. You could buy three or four BETTER printers for that now, including one which prints in color.

Turn on, log in, drop out

Okay, so you've got your computer, printer, etc. Now, in case there's some old fogy out there like me reading this who thinks the Internet is something you wear on your head at night (you know who you are), there is one more thing you should have in your electronic toolbox. Now-a-days this is almost a necessity if you're a stay-at-home freelancer. You need to get Internet access.

The cheapest access is via dial-up through an Internet Service Provider, or ISP. The most well-known ones are America On-line (AOL) and MSN (MSN). You can subscribe to either one of these for ten to twenty-two dollars a month depending on the level of service for which you sign up. There are others less well known which don't cost as much and probably are just as good for the purposes for which you'll want to use it. Most ISP's will provide you with the software you need to get set-up to connect and run their service. You can find free AOL CD's just about anywhere – computer stores, super markets, drug stores, drunk tanks, airport restrooms. You name it, they're in there free for the taking.

Get the CD, stick it in your computer and follow the bouncing ball. They'll have you on-line in less than ten minutes. They make it an easy and painless process for even the most computerly-challenged individual.

The biggest trade-off with dial up services is that they're... well, dial-up services. Which means, your connection will be agonizingly slow and un-reliable. On a regular basis you'll invariably be right in the middle of some transaction, like paying your light bill – which took you two hours to get to that page – and the dude will cheerily say, "Goodbye," and log your posterior off, no if, ands, or butts (little wordplay there).

That's why I switched to high speed access through my cable company. In most areas you can choose between your phone company or your cable company to get high speed access. These services are commonly referred to as DSL or cable modem, respectively.

What does DSL stand for, you ask? It stands for Dang Serious Lipservice. *I don't know.* Ask your phone guy.

Anyway, in my area the cable modem is an extra forty bucks a month on my cable bill. That's twice what I was paying AOL, but well worth it in my humble opinion. Now I can stay logged on all day, zip from site to site rapidly, while listening to my favorite on-line radio station, and never miss a phone call. All serious (including you oxymoronic serious humor) writers should have high speed Internet access.

Having an office makes you official

If you don't have a writing room of your own with a closable lockable (strongly recommended) door, get one. World without end, amen. This is an absolute must for any writer, humor or otherwise. And this private room should come even before your choice of writing instruments.

For those of you who live alone, no sweat. You can write in your living room, bedroom, or even your bathroom, if you're so moved… so to speak.

But for those of us with spouses, children, other miscellaneous relatives, and/or pets, we need a place to isolate ourselves from them. You should be prepared to receive a lot of sarcastic comments, cold stares, and even some hurt feelings when you do this, but it's absolutely essential that you ignore them for the time you're closed off in your writing sanctuary. I find it's easy to massage the hurt feelings by supplying flowers. Our local grocer has a floral department where guys like me can invest five or six bucks every week to regain some good graces. This works well for guy writers, but I'm not sure what would work for you women who live with a male. I'm guessing probably sex. We don't require much. For any other live-in variations, that's out of the realm of my life experience, so I'm not qualified to advise you. As far as dealing with the sarcastic remarks and dirty looks, I just write that off to the cost of doing business as a writer.

Writing is fundamentally a mental exercise and as such requires a good deal of concentration. I could be wrong, but humor writing, it seems to me, requires a different degree of concentration than, say, your average romance, mystery, or adventure writing in that you have to reach down and find a measure of cleverness you wouldn't in other genres in order to reach that certain point of funniness. Half-hearted, interrupted attempts at humor are like a fart in a crowded elevator. Now I'm not saying writers of other genres don't pay their dues. Writing of any kind requires a lot of discipline, concentration, skill, and downright hard work. All writers have my undying respect. I just know first hand what you have to go through to write humor, and perhaps I appreciate it a little more. Romance writers could argue the same for certain aspects of their efforts, and I wouldn't disagree, nor belittle them for it.

Be that as it may, it's hard to attain any measure of concentration when someone asks you what sounds good for supper, or did you feed the dog, or where's the car keys, or "Allison spit on me!" or "Did not! Did too! Did not!"

It's easier to tolerate pets, especially dogs, because they mostly sleep. But even they can disrupt your trains with their scratching and licking. Or their barking fits when the trashmen come by, and occasional demands to be let out. Mine likes to get under my desk or lay on the air conditioner vent about which we spend a lot of time arguing.

So, get a room. Then gather up all your writing stuff, go there, close the door, lock it if you can, and write. And write. Then write some more.

Practice may not make perfect, but it sure edges you closer and closer to that ideal. The more you do it the closer you get, AND the easier it becomes. Of course, writing just for the sake of writing can be an exercise in futility if you don't know the fundamentals. That's why I say…

Writing humor ain't no license to not write good

While it's true we humor writers might, from time to time, deviate from normal practices and methods of grammar and spelling in order to achieve a certain comic effect, we should not forget that we are members of the respected guild of the wordsmith, and as such should try to adhere to all the rules for constructing the written language.

Now I don't mean to sound highfalutin here, because for one thing I don't really know what falutin is at any level, and for another, I don't always practice what I'm preach. You can probably find one or two examples in this book. But the main thing is, we must always try to improve our skills as a writer.

Just like a professional golfer we should constantly get out on the practice tee and hit a bucket or two so that we can work ever closer to perfecting our game. And to drill this analogy into the ground a little more, there are certain immutable rules the golfer must follow in order to hit the ball where it must go. For example, he must always use a club of some sort to hit the ball. Golf courses, both public and private insist on this. Just like our golfer, we may be able to hit the ball a long way, but if we're doing something to hook the ball into the woods or slice it into the irrigation pond, our striking ability is of little value. Control beats distance every time.

Let's say you think you can be to writing humor as Tiger Woods is to golf. Okay, there's nothing wrong with your confidence then. Like Tiger, you have immense talent and ability. Yet he would be the first to tell you he has many flaws; that he can, and does, slip back into bad habits. He would say he got to where he is by practicing and playing golf for most of his waking hours every day, and that the only way he's going to stay at his level is to pay attention to what he's doing – right and wrong – and to keep honing it. So, just like Tiger, you should keep working on your game as a writer, and you should also, just like Tiger, wear a red shirt on Sundays. I'm not sure how that will help you improve as a writer, but I figure it can't hurt. It seems to work for Tiger.

Golf is a game that is fraught with rules (Stick with me here. I know the metaphor is starting to wear thin but I DO have a point.). Some of the rules are stodgy; all are strict. However, golf is a game that welcomes imagination and downright demands creativity. The rules are flexible to a certain extent, but you still have to play within the boundaries of the rules.

So it is with writing. Despite the fact that the stuffiest, most traditional, most conservative, most Caucasian male, most prestigious golf club in America has a chairman named Hootie, writing well in English, just as playing golf, requires you to know and follow certain rules.

I'm not going to enumerate or elaborate on those rules here, because there are resources and people available to you who are far more qualified than I to do this.

One such resource is *The Elements of Style* by William Strunk and E. B. White. If you've read other books on writing no doubt each of them exhorted you to get this book. I'm no exception. It should be a part of every serious (and serious humor) writer's library. It's a little book – ninety and a half pages counting the introduction. You can read it in a couple of hours. You can go back and re-read it with a necessary highlighter in about double that time. You can re-re-read the highlights in about an hour. I recommend you do the first two reads at least once, and the re-re-read about once every two months thereafter. Surprisingly, it has a fair amount of humor written into it. Neither of the authors address humor writing directly, but their subtle nuggets provide good indirect studies in the technique of writing… well, subtle humor.

I've got a third edition which I bought back in the '80's. I think the current edition is the fourth. You can pick one up from Amazon.com or Barnes and Noble for about eight bucks, or you can get a used copy for next to nothing through a used bookseller like ABEBooks.com.

I keep my copy on my desk next to my keyboard, as much for comfort as for quick reference. It's sort of like my literary Teddy bear; however, I keep my real Teddy bear in my bottom left drawer for those times I feel the need to suck my thumb.

That greased pig called "Style"

The "Strunk and White," as it's commonly called, is a succinct little book of rules for writing in the English language. In its Introduction, E. B. White wrote that Professor Stunk's original forty-three page work was "his attempt to cut the vast tangle of English rhetoric down to size and write its rules and principles on the head of a pin." I'd say he did that, but the part of the book I re-read most often is Mr. White's contribution: Chapter V – An Approach to Style. In it White discusses writing style in its broader sense: "…in the sense of what is distinguished and distinguishing."

Like all God's chillin, all writers need a style, and I'm talking about a writing style, not whether you drive a Lexus or a pickup, or wear Armani, Gap, or Salvation Army. But what is it? And how do we get one?

Here's what White said about style:

> There is no satisfactory explanation of style, no infallible guide to good writing, no assurance that a person who thinks clearly will be able to write clearly, no key that unlocks the door, no inflexible rule by which the... writer may shape

> his course. He will often find himself steering by the stars that are disturbingly in motion.

And this…

> Style is an increment in writing. When we speak of Fitzgerald's style, we don't mean his command of the relative pronoun, we mean the sound his word make on paper. Every writer, by the way he uses the language, reveals something of his spirit, his habits, his capacities, his bias. This is inevitable as well as enjoyable. All writing is communication; creative writing is communication through revelation – it is the Self escaping into the open. No writer long remains incognito.

Don't think I can add anything to that; it would be presumptuous if I tried.

The other thing worth noting in Chapter V of "Elements" is the list of what White calls, "…some suggestions and cautionary hints that may help the beginner find his way to a satisfactory style." No sense in my explaining them all here in detail, but I do feel it would be worthwhile, in the scope of this book, to enumerate them. They pretty much stand alone, but if you want further exposition on each, I suggest you go to book. Better yet, I strongly recommend it.

1. Place yourself in the background.
2. Write in a way that comes naturally.
3. Work from a suitable design.
4. Write with nouns and verbs.
5. Revise and rewrite.
6. Do not overwrite.

7. Do not overstate.
8. Avoid the use of qualifiers.
9. Do not affect a breezy manner.
10. Use orthodox spelling.
11. Do not explain too much.
12. Do not construct awkward adverbs.
13. Make sure the reader knows who is speaking.
14. Avoid fancy words.
15. Do not use dialect unless your ear is good.
16. Be clear.
17. Do not inject opinion.
18. Use figures of speech sparingly.
19. Do not take shortcuts at the cost of clarity.
20. Avoid foreign languages.
21. Prefer the standard to the offbeat.

To be sure, I have mangled if not totally ignored several of these. Humor writing, at least *my* style of it (☺), lends itself to this abuse; however, as they stand they are, as E.B. says "suggestions and cautionary hints." Every writer should be mindful of these, especially numbers 2 and 6.

Here's what E. B. said specifically about humor:

> "On the whole, the humorist who contributes pleasure to a wide audience are the ones who create characters and tell tales, the ones who are story tellers at heart."

And also this:

"[Humor] need only speak the truth, and I notice it always does."

Every toolbox needs a drill

We've discussed some of the basic mechanics of writing; now we should focus on some of the routines.

Another excellent book you should have in your writer's toolkit is Stephen King's *On Writing* (Simon & Schuster, 2000). Not only is this book an incisive work on the art and craft of writing by one of America's most prolific (and successful) writers, it's also most entertaining.

On Writing is part memoir, part method manual, part autobiography written in the inimitable style of King. Like all his books, it's easy and fun to read. Unlike most of his books, it's (explicitly) instructive to any writer, humor, fiction, or otherwise.

While Stephen King isn't known for his humor writing and while there may be two, at the most three, of you out there who don't like Mr. King's style and genre, you can't argue with his success. That in itself should demand that we listen to what he has to say about how to do it (writing).

SK calls *On Writing* a "short" book, and by his standards, I suppose it is. Not counting his three forewords and two afterwards it's a mere 275 pages long. Not exactly an afternoon's reading as *The Elements of Style*.

He said, in his second forward, one very revealing thing: "This is a short book because most books about writing are filled with bull****."

DOH! Now my secret is out. However, I promise you this book will be less than 275 pages, and will have, if any, only one foreword. Of course, Stephen King can get away with this because… well, he's Stephen King. Stephen King is the Martha Stewart of writers. Stephen may say that Martha is the Stephen King of… of… whatever the heck she is. A marketer? She could stick a couple of twigs in a pile of dog poop, put a ribbon on it and people would buy it. People would buy thousands of them. (At this writing it hasn't yet been determined if she will have an opportunity to decorate the cells of her and her fellow inmates.) That's basically what Stephen King could do, and does, with his writing. I'm not saying that he writes dog poop, but his grocery list would sell a million copies. I'm betting it would also be very long, maybe even have a couple of forewords and afterwords.

I read *The Stand* back in the 70's when it was a trim four hundred page book. Now, after its re-do, it's thicker than the Congressional Record. Steve, read E. B. White's Reminder #6 – Do not overwrite. Steve, remember Professor Strunk's Rule #17 – Omit needless words.

Well, you and I should heed Reminder 6 and Rule 17, even if SK doesn't have to. A market economy doesn't require brevity in popular fiction, nor sanity in home decorations.

Meet my companions, the twins – Fear & Doubt

Another thing King said in this book is, "I'm convinced that fear is the root of most bad writing."

I can certainly relate to that, and I bet you can too. Many is the time I've sat down to write only to have that old demon Fear and his cohort Doubt come into the room and snigger at me. “What’re you doing, loser,” one will say. “Trying to write again?”

“Yeah, you’re a big dumb stupidhead,” says the other. “No one’s going to want to read what you write. Watch my lips – You can’t write. Writing is hard. You just don’t have what it takes.”

“Besides,” chimes in Fear. “The editors you send this crap to won’t like you. They have piles of stuff from good writers. You’re tripe will only piss them off. Rejection! Rejection! Rejection!”

“Yeah,” echoes Doubt. “You should go watch some TV or go eat something. Better yet, go to a movie. It’s dark in there. You won’t have to worry about us being there.”

So it goes. You’d think they’d get tired of the same old routine everyday, but they don’t. So I’ve come up with this habit which helps me ignore them until they get bored and go away for awhile. I figure the more I do this the less time they’ll waste with me. Also, my medication helps.

The continuing saga of yours truly

Second thing after I get up every morning I go into the kitchen and drink a glass of orange juice, eat a banana, and pour myself a cup of coffee. Well, that’s more like four things, but then I head to my office, settle down at my desk, and before I read e-mail, before I roam the Internet, before I do anything else, I write in my journal. I don’t permit myself to do any other activity until I’ve made my personal journal entry for the day.

I am very obsessive-compulsive about this because it sets the tone for my day of writing. It’s like a runner who goes through a series of stretching exercises before he sets off on his jaunt.

I write my journal as if I never intend for anyone to ever read it. In fact, I've password protected the file so that NO ONE but me CAN read it. And I rarely go back and read past entries. I used to think my journals were golden and someday someone would discover them, and like the Dead Sea Scrolls, they would end up in a museum for scholars to pore over. With such thinking, I became frozen with fear at not writing brilliant things in my journals, which eventually prevented me from writing in them altogether.

I finally realized that my journals are just a place for me to ramble. Maybe there's something brilliant there, maybe not. The main thing is that it's a warming up exercise. It not only loosens up the finger joints, but it gets the brain juices flowing too.

By telling myself I will delete this journal file sometime on down the road, I lose the inhibition to write freely, as the spirit moves me. That's not to say that I don't pay attention to structure, grammar, spelling, and that mysterious butterfly called style. That's all part of improving my skills as a writer, so I have to pay attention to them; but by writing freely and without psychological constraint, I hope to eventually master the mechanics so that they become second nature.

I do have, however, a certain strict format I follow in making my daily entries. There's nothing magical about how I set up each entry. It just suits my personal motivation and style. It's sort of a Captain Kirk (or Picard for you Next Genners) Star Log Entry type. You should do your entries in the way that best works for you.

So, just as an example, here's how I set up my journal:

Besides my usual daily header of date, time, day, weather, temperature, and precipitation amount (I'm what kind of retentive, you say?), I start every entry by writing the last verse of Psalm 19:

"May the words of my mouth and the meditations of my heart be acceptable in Your sight, O Lord, my Strength and Redeemer."

I start out this way for three reasons – 1. I know exactly how I'm going to start writing every day. No sitting staring at the screen. 2. It starts everything off on a positive note. 3. It suits me to begin my writing day with a prayer.

I'm a fan of classical music. I once heard that the great composer Franz Joseph Haydn, when asked how he wrote such beautiful music, said, "Before I start, I pray to God that I will have divine guidance, and I write the music until I have it."

Now, admittedly, I'm no Haydn, but to me the principle is sound.

The next thing I do is write out my goals. Dr. Phil (no relation) McGraw once said all successful people have four common attributes: Well-defined goals, a clear vision, unrestrained passion for what they do, and lots of energy. I write my goals every day, so that I will always keep them in front of me, so that they will become a part of my conscious and unconscious thought. I set my goals as specifically as I can. My personal and professional goals are one and the same as far as I'm concerned, both the mundane and lofty. I write them in a list of single concise sentences starting with "I will…"

1. I will write for the glory of God every day.

2. I will write at least 1,000 words a day.
3. I will complete my humor book by June 1, 2003.
4. I will write and sell an article a month in 2003.
5. I will make $X in 2003.
6. I will brush my teeth at least twice every day.
7. I will…

When I reach a goal, I replace it with another. I stick mostly to short-range goals – those within a year, two at the most; but writing one's long-range goals (five years or greater) probably isn't a bad idea either. Individual preference, I'd say. Personally, I have a hard time looking beyond two years.

After my goals, I write my vision, that is, the things I see myself doing, not only to accomplish my goals, but as a result of reaching them. I write these in a paragraph with each sentence starting, "I see myself…"

I see myself working every day to improve my skills as a writer and speaker. I see myself in book stores signing my books. I see myself opening envelopes containing checks for my writing…

I once heard a line in a movie (this is a paraphrase): "Everything that exists in our world was first imagined." I don't want to get all philosophical and Zen-ish, but that is a most powerful and absolute truth. Think about it. Nothing, not a table, not a chair, not a building, not a nuclear bomb, not a bridge, not a symphony, not a painting, not a lunar lander, not a cathedral, not a child, not a book existed until it was first imaged, pictured, seen. Therefore, the logical place to start with your dream is to imagine it in as much detail as you can, and then to keep that image, that vision, in front of you.

Sorry to sound like an Amway leader, but truth is truth whether it's about soap or philosophy. And I write my vision down every day just like my goals to burn them into my brain. This technique of writing my goals and vision every day is something I adopted from a couple of sources. Several years ago I read an interview with Scott Adams in which he espoused writing your goals down fifteen times a day. He claims it works like magic. I don't know if it's magic or not, but I do know writing your goals down seems to carve a pathway into your thinking and attitude, and the more you do it, the more beaten down that pathway becomes. Fifteen times a day is a little tedious, I think, but my routine of starting my journal entries with them every morning, works well for me.

As for the vision thing, that works more or less the same way. Many years ago I read a book by Norman Vincent Peale called *Dynamic Imaging* in which he said that if you image yourself in a situation, that is, "see" yourself there, it will eventually come true. This is a little weird, I know. Sort of a Dorothy Clicking the Heels of the Ruby Slippers exercise, but if you read the book it'll make sense. Dr. Peale was no snake oil salesman. He was and is an icon of positive thinking. There is definite power in positive thinking. Book stores have whole sections dedicated to volumes written about it.

It's like Chicken Writer says, "If you don't have a dream, you're probably a chicken." Setting goals and having a vision are important, but they don't go anywhere unless you work at them. You won't have a compulsion to do that until you take them out and look at them every day.

Okay, so you've got the goals, you've got the vision, you write them every day so you won't forget them. Now what do you have to do to write and sell humor. Start with…

Phil's First Dozen Rules for Humor Writing

The following rules aren't totally original, but they are true. They're more or less a compilation of things I've learned, mostly the hard way, in nearly four decades of trying to earn money writing. I try to keep these rules hard and fast, and recommend you do the same.

1. Don't write for free

This should be every writer's number one rule. Early in my writing career I was held captive by some monthly and weekly publications who liked my columns well enough to publish them, but not enough to pay me for them. I went along because I was, one – young and naïve; two – thought they would eventually see the value in my writing and start paying me (see naïve above); three – was happy with the byline. The ego massage of seeing your name in print only lasts for so long. I realize getting credits is part of the writing game, and contributor's copies are all well and good, but the hard cold truth is, no mortgage company cares a whit about your tear sheets.

Seek paying markets and do the work necessary to sell and get paid for what you write. You just have to learn to bow your neck and forge ahead. You will get many rejections, but it beats giving it away, which is like kissing your sister.

2. Write clean

It seems to be the current trend to write and speak with a liberal application of four letter words. Books, movies, stand-up comics all do this. It's even creeping steadily into prime time TV shows. In *On Writing* Stephen King advocates writing this way, arguing that this is the way people talk and you should write how people talk. I disagree. I don't talk that way, and I don't believe one has to talk or write that way to be a good writer. I feel that clean humor is the best humor. For one thing you appeal to a much broader audience, but more importantly, I don't think anyone is served by crude and vulgar writing. Anyone can write obscenities, but I don't see how that adds to the humor. To me, it's low-class, vulgar, un-creative, un-inspired, and lazy. Swear words and obscenities degrade the language that serves you as a writer, and you personally as an English speaking/writing member of society. If you must write swear words, do it in French. They look and sound much better than their English equivalents. Besides, the French have no couth anyway. My rule of thumb: Never write anything your grandmother wouldn't read. (And my grandmother was pretty cool.)

3. Write a lot

For any kind of writer, humor writers included, the most fundamental, basic rule to achieving writing success is this three word rule. You may have noticed my second goal is that I will write AT LEAST 1,000 words a day. That is my minimum goal, not counting emails and grocery lists. It's a simple rule. The more you write the better you get at it.

4. Read a lot

If you don't read in general, you won't learn to read better or write better. I can't tell you how many people enter our writing contests who don't read the rules. I love these people. I love them because it's easy money. If they don't follow the rules, they go directly into the "Nope" stack without a read. At the same time I wonder how can they expect to write, if they can't or don't read. Besides being better able to follow written rules or directions, reading only makes you a better writer because you're more in tune to the written language. Reading is fundamental. It's the reason we write. This could be rule 1b.

5. Re-write and revisit your revisions.

If you haven't already, write down William Strunk's Rule 17: "Omit needless words" on a sticky note and place it on the front of your computer screen so you can see it as you write. If you don't use a computer, stick it on the back of the hand you write with. Better yet, do both of the above. You might even consider putting said sticky note on your bathroom mirror, but that's entirely up to you.

Revising is tough. I'd say it's the most difficult writing skill to learn to use. You look at 1,000-word piece you've just done and it's perfect. You say, "How can I cut anything out? To do so would ruin it." But when a magazine wants a 750-word piece, you have no choice. I have found that this kind of requirement makes me a better writer. It forces me to snip and trim and massage my writing. Generally, when it's done I find it a much more attractive and readable version. Now, I almost look forward the re-write/revising step in my writing. I think it was Michelangelo who, when asked how he created such beautiful sculptures, answered, "I just cut away all the marble which isn't part of the sculpture until it's finished." So true, Mike.

One other thing I should mention here is to put some time between your first draft and your first revision. Every author of every book on how to write makes this statement, and I agree. We writers, in the heat of writing passion, get so enamored with our stuff that we can't see the flaws.

I'm put in mind of my first time(s) I fell in love. That first week or two when we were together (almost constantly) the woman of my dreams had such a golden glow about her that I saw no failing. She made me sing, she made me dance, she made me laugh. Her face and hair and her… uh, the rest of her was a work of art. I was thrilled; she was perfect. Then I went away for a while – to college, the Army, Dallas. When I came back, a little older, a little wiser; I noticed she talked with a really shrill voice when she got excited, and she would snort when she laughed, and that mole on her neck had a hair growing out of it. Where did that come from? And I never knew she didn't like Credeence Clearwater for Pete's sake! So one night I called her and, before I could say what I wanted to say, she said, "Phil, I've been thinking… it's just… well, maybe we should start seeing other people."

My point is, it's generally a good rule not to declare something you've written finished in less than two weeks after it's inception. And the same rule would apply to taking that certain someone home to meet the folks. Write it, let it lay fallow for a few days or a few weeks, then go back and re-read it. Chances are about 99% you'll see much about it you can cut, change, or make better.

7. Be yourself

You're probably saying to yourself, "Duh. Be yourself. You think?" However obvious this rule may seem, many of us have a tendency to take on another persona when we write. See E. B. White's suggestion Number 9 – "Do not affect a breezy manner." You're entirely distinctive and uncopied. Unless you're Dolly the cloned sheep, or live in Arkansas, you're DNA is uniquely yours. You are one in several billion. When people read what you've written they should see that, not some poor, half-baked imitation of Dave Barry or Bill Cosby or Newt Gingrich. You have much to offer as a writer, so give it.

8. Remember grammar and spelling.

Although I take a lot of liberties with grammar and spelling, I do it all in the name of humor. Of course, one of the beauties of writing humor is that you can always claim that screwed up spelling and grammar, was no mistake, that it was all part of your plan. You can then turn the tables on your critic(s) and make them feel stupid for not seeing the humor in it. This is a great trapdoor for the humor writer, from which we can deftly escape the grammar police, but it's still better to follow the established rules of the written language. Knowing and using proper grammar and spelling is what sets us, as writers, apart from the great unwashed, by which I mean the French.

9. Don't force it.

Sometimes we have a tendency to over-sell a story in our narrative. We think we need to explain more so that our readers will understand why it's so funny. If we think we have to keep adding to our story to help the reader understand why it's funny, it probably wasn't funny to begin with. Or it could have been funny to begin with, and we just wouldn't let it stand on its own. This is where we need to develop some of these comedy writing skills:

Brevity – fewer words are better than more words.

Rhythm and Timing – Formally defined as a sense of temporal development, these are elusive attributes. Reading, writing, and experience help you acquire these.

Rhyme – See limericks, Ogden Nash, Dr. Suess.

Repetition – Using a word or phrase two or more times to get a laugh, e.g., She said, "What's that in the road ahead?" He said, "What's that in the road? A head?" Okay, a weak example, but the technique of repetition needs to be in context, and requires good timing.

Juxtaposition and the Non Sequitur – Juxtaposing places two or more things together for comparison, and the non sequitur is a statement that does not follow logically from what preceded it. For example, "American humorists have much in common with their French counterparts. For instance, who doesn't get a big laugh from Dave Barry, Bill Cosby, Donald Rumsfeld, and at the same time, Jacques Chirac's nose."

10. Take criticism

As a writer, if you don't have thick skin, you should get some. If you've been writing for a while, you've probably found this out. Just like jerks, there's no shortage of critics in the world. I had a critic the minute I popped into the world. The first time I ever wrote anything I got criticized.

"Phil, Don't write on the walls with that crayon!" my mother said. Then, SMACK!

I started developing a tough hide on my posterior. I had plenty of experience. But getting critiqued on your writing is about as important as revising. In fact, criticism aids in revision.

Here's some criticism to all of us humor writers from Stephen King:

> "Informal essays are, by and large, silly and insubstantial things; unless you get a job as a columnist at your local newspaper, writing such fluffery is a skill you'll never use in the actual mall-and-filling station world..."

My first reaction to that is, "Right, Steve. At least we have enough sense to get out of the way of traffic." But that's a mean thing to say (see Rule 12). Besides, his criticism is not entirely wrong. Plenty of columns I have written are silly, and no doubt most are insubstantial, and I sure haven't found many laying around in filling stations and malls. However, that won't stop me from setting that goal and doggedly working to achieve it. We'd still be living in caves and eating the mulberries instead of painting the walls with them if we would have quit after all our peers told us how wrong our endeavors were and why we shouldn't do them. Criticism should fan a fire in you, not blow out the flame. First of all, believe in yourself and what you can do, then put the criticism to good use.

Here's another thing Steve said, which, frankly, surprised me:

> "If God gave you something you can do, why in God's name wouldn't you do it."

Couldn't have said it better myself, you rich and famous scary story writer monkey.

11. Don't write in a vacuum.

Somewhere back in my formal education, I took a writing course in which the instructor said this. I think it was in one of those opening monologues academic types like to present the first class session, and then leave to let their frazzle-haired grad assistants take over for the rest of the semester. I don't remember much else about the course, but this has stuck with me all these years. Back then, sometime in my early twenties, I didn't know much, so I didn't write much. And what I did write wasn't that well informed. Now, almost two score years, two marriages, one war, two children, and several close encounters with working in corporate America, my life experience knowledge base is anything but airless.

Experiencing life is paramount to being a writer, but you also need to associate with your peers and colleagues on a regular basis. Now that I no longer participate in the fun and games down at the office, I find it very easy to sit in my writing room all day, listen to Mozart, eat Snackwell's devil's food cookies, drink Diet Cokes and write. Not healthy, physically or mentally. If you find yourself doing the same thing, my suggestion here is that you should join local writers' groups and critique groups, go to writers' conventions and writers' seminars. In fact, you should do this even if you still occupy real estate in Cubesville. It's important that you mix regularly with your own phylum so you can share and see and hear what's going on in the writing world. Who knows, you might even get lucky… and meet an editor or publisher who want you to send them something.

Oh, and it would also probably be a good idea to get some exercise. And walking from your computer to the kitchen doesn't count. I mean working out somehow, be it in a gym, a walk around the block, pick-up basketball, chasing after rainbows, whatever. Physical exercise puts oxygen in your body and brain, which gives you more energy, which helps you serve the passion for your dreams, your vision.

12. Write with a positive spirit.

There is a fine line between satirizing someone or some group and being downright mean. It's like our mothers said, "Laugh with someone, not at them."

Admittedly, I don't adhere to this rule as much as I should. My occasional jabs at the French being a case in point. But I don't write hate. Venomous, negative writing isn't beneficial to anyone. Venom you inject means there's venom inside you to start with, so the only one you poison is yourself. I try to approach all my writing - as much as possible - with a constructive, optimistic, unbigoted and upbeat attitude. I feel this will bring me a much greater and closer following than the opposite. Of course, the French get in the way a lot.

Bringing it on Home

The Gospel

One of the pitfalls of writing a book like this is running the risk of preaching. There are two things writers should know about preachy writing: don't do it, but if you do, practice it. I'm afraid I've sinned mightily in both of these areas.

I like what E. B. White said concerning his Suggestion 17 – Do not inject opinion:

> "To air one's views gratuitously... is to imply that the demand for them is brisk, which may not be the case..."

Beautifully understated and wry, as usual. However, books on how to do something, especially the one's on writing, proceed on the premise that someone (with any luck many thousands of someones) want know what you have to say on the subject, and will actively (using cash or credit card) seek your views. That in itself holds a certain arrogance and conceit, which is okay if you're a journalism major because your daddy paid dearly for you to take several college courses dealing with those important professional skills. If you were an English major, like me, you disdained those kinds of establishment teachings and learned arrogance and conceit on your own.

In either case, writing, which includes the eventuality of your turning to writing about writing, carries with it many pieces of luggage containing all the things there are about you the person. As we discussed in the section on style, you should be yourself when you write; that style is, in fact, an abstract painting of you. Hopefully, you're not Saddam Hussein or one of his boys, because your style would not be very appealing. On the other hand, if you were Baghdad

Bob, your style would be hilarious and at the same time a little sad, assuming you could feel sadness for any of those creeps. Still, you would probably sell a lot of books, because for the most part people like to hear and read the words of fools.

So it's okay to bring a little arrogance and conceit when you sit down at the writing table. You know things and have experienced things, and they are all unique because they happened to you. Others may have had similar experiences, but no one has had YOUR experiences. That's what should make your writing unique and original.

In Summation, let's add things up

If you truly want to write humor, then go ahead and make a fool of yourself. I won't stop you. It's probably not what your parents had in mind for you, but you wouldn't be the first person to break your poor old folks' hearts. Personally, I recommend that you stick to selling glue, photocopying your fanny, or whatever it is you do on a regular basis to keep your creditors and the IRS happy. However, if you're like me (you poor devil), you probably never have been very good at listening to sound advice, so let's go over some of the major points I brought up in this book. If you pay attention to them, maybe you too can eventually enjoy the benefits and prestige that comes with making $100 a year writing humor.

First, stay in school and don't take (too many) drugs.

Second, write like it is going out of style, which in some cases it is. If you learn to write computer code for video games, or questions for TV bachelorettes and/or bachelors to ask their contestants, you'll probably do okay.

Humor on the printed page will most likely become a quaint curiosity.

Third, get serious about your humor writing. Study the craft of the masters, practice by emulating them, read what they've written over and over again. Most importantly, take pride in what you do and don't pay attention to those who say writing humor is not important or is "fluffery." It's as significant to the reading world as, say, any story about a telekinetic psychotic teenager who sets fire to her peer on prom night.

Fourth, don't keep what you've written stuffed away in folders on your hard drive. Find people who say they're looking for humor writing – especially those who say they'll pay to get it – and send some to them. Even though all editors have pointed teeth, horns, and a pitchfork, don't be afraid of them. Even though you will be summarily rejected ninety percent of the time, sometimes you will get small hand-written critiques. Use those rare suggestions and take heart in them. If an editor takes the time to scrawl something on your manuscript before sending it back to you, it means you wrote something worthy of her attention. But even when you don't, learn from what you do and the way you do it and build on that. Submitting your work is a tedious and heavily discouraging process, but persistence usually pays off. Like anything else, the more you do it, the better you get at it. And once you start making a few sales, the process gets easier.

Fifth, analyze what you write and see if you can't make it better. Cut out needless words; look at a sentence with a passive verb and re-word it with an action verb to see how much more power it gives your writing; don't consider anything you've written carved in stone, unless, of course, you happen to be a person who does tombstones.

Sixth, write humor because you love it and can't stop, no matter what your friends and relatives say. Don't quit; don't give up. There are so many things in the world that are absolutely **NOT** funny, so people like you and I must write humor. It's a sacred duty… or perhaps, it's a sack of doody. I forget which.

Off to the Market to Sell a Fat Pig

Where the rubber meets the Chicken

Right about now, assuming you've read the preceding hundred odd pages – some odder than others [rim shot!] – you're probably saying to yourself, "Okay, talk is cheap. Cut to the chase and tell me where I should send this stuff."

That being said, here's some suggested markets for your humor. This is by no means a definitive list, and I can't guarantee some have changed formats, addresses, or gone belly up since I put this together, but it will give you an idea of where to look. Remember to use your market search tools, such as Writers Market (on-line and print) and WritingforDOLLARS.COM, to find out where and how to send your material. Needless to say, you should study the publication before submitting anything. Most of these publications have on-line writer's guidelines, but I've included their mailing addresses as well as their Home and Guidelines URL (Internet address, for those of you who are French).

You can also find information on these publications from the on-line guidelines page on Writingfordollars.com – http://www.writingfordollars.com/Guidelines.cfm

Levels of payment are defined as:

L$: Large Bucks – over $500.

M$: Medium Bucks – from $150-$500.

S$: Small Bucks – less than $150.

Consumer Magazines

AAA Going Places: S$, 50% freelance, pays on publication. Seeks nonfiction on travel destinations, domestic and international. Subjects: historical, how-to, humor, personal experience, interviews, travel.

No Web site.

Send for guidelines.

AAA Going Places
AAA Auto Club South
1515 N. Westshore Blvd.
Tampa, FL 33607

The Atlantic Monthly: L$, pays on acceptance. Seeks nonfiction, fiction, fillers. Subjects: Book excerpts, essays, general interest, humor, personal experience, religious, travel, poetry.

Home page: http://www.theatlantic.com

Guidelines:
http://www.theatlantic.com/letters/edlet.htm

The Atlantic Monthly
77 North Washington St.
Boston, MA 02114

A&U – American AIDS Magazine: L$, 50% freelance, pays on publication. Seeks nonfiction columns, fiction, photo essays. Subjects: essays, general opinion, how-to, humor, personal experience, interviews, travel.

Home: http://www.aumag.org

Guidelines:
http://www.aumag.org/contactus/submit.html

America's AIDS Magazine
Art & Understanding, Inc.
25 Monroe St. Suite 205
Albany NY 12210-2729

Adventure Cylist: M$, 75% freelance, pays on publication. Seeks: non-fiction. Subjects: How-To, Humor, Interview/Profile, Photo Feature, Technical,Travel.

Web site: http://www.adv-cycling.org

Send for guidelines.

Adventure Cycling Assn.
Box 8308
Missoula, MT 59807

Air & Space Magazine: L$, 80% freelance, pays on acceptance. 80% freelance. Seeks:, non-fiction, photos, columns. Needs: Book excerpts, Essays, General Interest (on aviation/aerospace), Historical, humor, Photo Feature, Technical

Web site: www.airspacemag.com

Guidelines:
http://www.airandspacemagazine.com/asm/mag/WritersGuide.html

Smithsonian Institution
P.O. Box 37012

Victor Bldg. 7100, MRC 951
Washington, DC 20013-7012

Backpacker: L$, pays on acceptance. 50% freelance. Seeks: non-fiction, photos, columns. Needs: Essays, Historical, How-To, Humor, Inspirational, Interview/Profile, New Product, Personal Experience, Technical, Travel.

Web site: www.backpacker.com

Guidelines: http://www.backpacker.com/guidelines

Rodale
33 E. Minor St.
Emmaus, PA 18098-0099

Baltimore Magazine: M$, 60% freelance, pays on acceptance. Seeks nonfiction, columns/departments, photos/artwork. Subjects: Baltimore, essays, expose, humor, interview/profile , personal experience, photo feature, travel.

Web site: http://www.baltimoremagazine.net

Guildelines:
http://www.baltimoremagazine.net/writer_guidelines.htm

Baltimore magazine
Inner Harbor East • 1000 Lancaster Street, Suite 400
Baltimore, Maryland 21202

Boca Raton Magazine: L$, 70% freelance, pay on acceptance. Seeks non-fiction, reprints, photos, columns. Subjects: South Florida general interest, historical, humor, interview/profile, photo feature, travel.

Web site: http://www.bocamag.com

Send for guidelines.

JES Publishing
6413 Congress Ave. Suite 100
Boca Raton, FL 33487

Chicago Magazine: L$, 50% freelance, pays on acceptance. Seeks: non-fiction Chicago oriented. Subjects: exposé, humor, personal experience.

Web site: http://www.chicagomag.com

Send for guidelines.

500 N. Dearborn, Suite 1200
Chicago, IL 60610-4901

Christian Parenting Today: M$, 90% freelance, pays on acceptance. Seeks non-fiction, reprints, columns. Needs: book excerpts, how-to, humor, inspirational, religious.

Web site:
http://www.christianitytoday.com/parenting

Guidelines:
http://www.christianitytoday.com/parenting/features/info.html

Christianity Today International
465 Gundersen Dr.
Carol Stream, IL 60188-2489

Cruising World: L$, 60% freelance, pays on acceptance. Seeks non-fiction, reprints, columns. Subjects: essays, exposé, general interest, historical, how-to, humor, opinion, personal experience.

Web site: http://www.cruisingworld.com

Guidelines:
http://www.cruisingworld.com/cw_contact.php

The Sailing Co.
5 John Clarke Rd.
Newport, RI 02840-0992

Dialogue: S$, 60% freelance, pays on publication. Seeks nonfiction, fiction, fillers. Subjects: of interest/assistance to newly blind, career and leisure experiences, fiction, humor, and poetry.

Web site: http://www.blindskills.com

Guidelines: http://www.blindskills.com/submit.html

Blindskills, Inc.
P.O. 5181
Salem, OR 97304-0181

The Door: M$, 90% freelance, pays on publication. Seeks nonfiction. Subjects: exposé, humor, interview/profile, religious.

Home: http://thedoormagazine.com

Guidelines:
http://thedoormagazine.com/wguidelines.html

The *Door* Editorial Offices
P.O. Box 1444
Waco, TX 76703-1444

Easyriders Magazine: M$, 50% freelance, pay on publication Seeks non-fiction, fiction. Subjects: general interest, historical, how-to, humor, inspirational, interview/profile, opinion, personal experience, photo feature, technical, motorcycle travel.

Web site: http://www.easyriders.net

Send for guidelines.

Paisano Publications, Inc.
P.O. Box 3000
Agoura Hills, CA 91301

Family Circle Magazine: L$, 80% freelance, pays on acceptance. Seeks: non-fiction, columns, women oriented. Subjects: essays, humor, opinion, personal experience.

Web site:
http://www.familycircle.com/home/homepage.jsp

Send for guidelines.

Gruner & Jahr
375 Lexington Ave.
New York, NY 10017-5514

First Opportunity: M$, 80% freelance, pays on publication. Seeks non-fiction, reprints, columns, fiction, fillers. Subjects: general interest, how-to (dealing with careers or education), humor, inspirational, interview/profile (celebrity or), personal experience.

No Web site.

Send for guidelines.

Communications Publishing Group
3100 Broadway, Suite 660
Kansas City, MO 64111

Frontier: L$, 50% freelance , pays on publication. Accepts simultaneous submissions. Seeks nonfiction, columns/departments, photos/artwork. Subjects: Essays, General Interest, Historical, Humor, Interview, Photo Feature, Travel.

Home: http://www.frontiermag.com

Guidelines: http://www.frontiermag.com/forms.html

Adventure Media
3983 S. McCarran Blvd.
No. 434
Reno, NV 89502

Guideposts for Kids: M$, 90% freelance , pays on acceptance. Seeks nonfiction, fiction, columns/departments, fillers, photos/artwork. Subjects: children 7-12, general interest, humor, inspirational.

Home: http://www.gp4k.com

Guidelines:
http://www.gp4k.com/frontpage/guidelines.asp

Guideposts for Kids
1050 Broadway, Ste. 6
Chesterton, IN 46304

Guideposts for Teens: M$, 90% freelance , pays on acceptance. Seeks nonfiction, columns/departments, fillers. Subjects: teenagers 12-18, true stories, humor.

No Web site.

Send for guidelines.

Guideposts for Teens
P.O. Box 638
Chesterton, IN 46304

It's All Happening at the Zoo!: S$, pays on publication. Seeks nonfiction. Subjects: Business humor.

No Web site.

Send for guidelines.

It's All Happening at the Zoo!
P.O. Box 74
Riverbank, CA 95367

Steve Herbelin, editor

I love Cats: S$, 100% freelance, pays on publication. Seeks: non-fiction, fiction, fillers (about cats). Subjects: essays, general interest, how-to, humor, inspirational.

Web site: http://www.iluvcats.com

Guidelines:
http://www.iluvcats.com/writguidfori.html

I Love Cats Publishing
16 Meadow Hill Lane
Armonk, NY 10504

The International: L$, 70% freelance, pays on publication. Seeks men's non-fiction, columns, fillers. Subjects: exposé, general interest, historical, humor, interview/profile, opinion, personal experience.

No Web site.

Send for guidelines.

Tomorrow Enterprises
2228 E. 20th St.
Oakland, CA 94606

Jacksonville: M$, 50% freelance, pays on publication. Seeks non-fiction, reprints, columns. Subjects: historical, humor, interview/profile, opinion, personal experience.

No Web site.

Send for guidelines.

White Publishing Co.
1032 Hendricks Ave.
Jacksonville FL 32207

Keynoter: M$, 65% freelance, pays on acceptance. Seeks non-fiction, reprints. Subjects: historical, humor, interview/profile, opinion.

Web site: http://www.keyclub.org

Guidelines:
http://www.keyclub.org/BeInformed/ClubResources/spotlight.html

Key Club International
3636 Woodview Trace
Indianapolis, IN 46268-3196

Lake Country Journal Magazine: M$, 90% freelance, pays on publication. Seeks non-fiction, columns, fiction. Subjects: essays, general interest, humor, interview/profile, how-to, personal experience.

Web site: http://www.lakecountryjournal.com

Guidelines:
http://www.lakecountryjournal.com/submissions.html

Evergreen Press of Brainerd
P.O. Box 465
Brainerd, MN 56401

Latin Trade: L$, 55% freelance, pays on publication. Seeks non-fiction covering Latin business. Subjects: expose, historical, humor, interview/profile, travel, business news.

Web site:
http://www.latintrade.com/newsite/news/magazine.cfm

Send for guidelines.

95 Merrick Way
Suite 600
Coral Gables, FL 33134

Marriage Partnership: L$, 50% freelance , pays on publication. Seeks nonfiction, columns/departments. Subjects: Marriage how-to pieces; interviews with experts; humorous articles; true-life stories.

Home: http://www.christianitytoday.com/marriage

Guidelines:
http://www.christianitytoday.com/marriage/features/writers

Christianity Today International
465 Gundersen Dr.
Carol Stream, IL 60188

Montana Magazine: M$, 50% freelance , pays on publication. Accepts simultaneous submissions. Seeks nonfiction, columns/departments, photos/artwork. Subjects: Montana recreation, contemporary issues, people, natural history, cities, towns, humor, wildlife

Home: http://www.montanamagazine.com

Guidelines:
http://www.montanamagazine.com/submit/submitguides.html

Montana Magazine
P.O. Box 5630
Helena, MT 59604

MyBusiness Magazine: M-L$, 75% freelance, pays on acceptance. Seeks non-fiction on small business. Subjects: book excerpts, how-to, humor.

Web site: http://www.mybusinessmag.com

Guidelines:
http://www.mybusinessmag.com/about/guide.php

Hammock Publishing
3322 W. End Ave. Suite 700
Nashville, TN 37203

New Humor: S$, 90% freelance, pays on publication. Accepts simultaneous submissions. Seeks nonfiction, fiction, fillers. Subjects: humor.

No Web site.

Send for guidelines.

New Humor
P.O. Box 216
Lafayette, PA 19444

The Old Farmer's Almanac: L$, 95% freelance, pays on acceptance. Seeks non-fiction, fillers. Subjects: general interest, historical, how-to, humor.

Web site: http://www.almanac.com/index.php

Guidelines:
http://www.almanac.com/guidelines/index.php

Yankee Publishing, Inc.
Main St.
Dublin, NH 03444

Pet Life: M$, 85% freelance, pays on publication. Seeks: non-fiction, fillers. Subjects: pet-human bond related humor, inspirational, interview/profile, personal experience.

Web site: http://www.petlifeweb.com.

Send for guidelines.

Magnolia Media Group
3451 Boston Ave.
Fort Worth, TX 76116

Players: M$, 40% freelance, pays on publication. Seeks nonfiction, columns/departments, photos/artwork. Subjects: humor, social issues, sports, fiction, and health for black men.

No Web site.

Send for guidelines.

PLAYERS MAGAZINE
8060 Melrose Avenue
Los Angeles, CA 900462

Reader's Digest: M-L$, freelance specific depts., pays on acceptance. Seeks non-fiction, reprints, columns. Subjects: general interest, historical, how-to, inspirational, humor.

Web site: http://www.rd.com

Guidelines: click on **Submit a Joke** button on Home page.

Reader's Digest Rd.
Pleasantville, NY 10570-7000

Road King: M$, 25% freelance, pays on acceptance. Seeks nonfiction, columns/departments, fillers, photos/artwork. Subjects: trucking, drivers and their rigs, equipment, history, travel destinations, humor.

Web site: http://www.roadking.com

Send for guidelines.

Hammock Publishing
3322 West End

Avenue, Suite 700
Nashville, TN 37203

The Rotarian: L$, 40% freelance, pays on acceptance. Seeks non-fiction, reprints. Subjects: general interest, humor, inspirational, travel, sports.

Web site: http://www.rotary.org

Send for guidelines.

Rotary International
1560 Sherman Ave.
Evanston, IL 60201-4818

Sports Illustrated for Kids: High paying market , pays on acceptance. Seeks nonfiction, columns/departments, photos/artwork. Subjects: games, general interest, how-to, humor, inspirational, interview/profile, photo feature, puzzles.

No Web site.

Send for guidelines.

SPORTS ILLUSTRATED FOR KIDS
1271 Avenue of the Americas
4th Floor
New York, NY 10020

Troika: M$, 95% freelance, pays on publication. Seeks non-fiction, reprints, columns, fiction. Subjects: essays, expose, general interest, inspirational, how-to, humor.

Web site: http://www.troikamagazine.com

Send for guidelines.

Lone Tout Publications, Inc.
P.O. Box 1006
Weston, CT 06883

UMM (Urban Male Magazine): M$, 100% freelance, pays on publication. Seeks non-fiction, fillers. Subjects: expose, general interest, historical, how-to, humor.

Web site: http://www.umm.ca

Send for guidelines.

UMM Publishing Inc.
70 George St. Suite 200
Ottawa, ON K1N 5V9
Canada

Virginia Quarterly Review: S$, mostly freelance, pays on publication. Seeks nonfiction, fiction, columns/departments, fillers. Subjects: Book excerpts, essays, general interest, historical/nostalgic, humor, inspirational.

Web site: http://www.virginia.edu/vqr

Guidelines:
http://www.virginia.edu/vqr/guidelines.html

Editorial Offices:

One West Range
Box 400223
Charlottesville, VA 22904-4223
vqreview@virginia.edu

Whole Life Times: S$, 50% freelance , pays on publication. Seeks nonfiction, columns/departments, photos/artwork. Subjects: Healing, Parenting, Finance, Food, Personal Growth, Relationships, Humor, Travel, Psychology.

No Web site.

Whole Life Times
P.O. Box 1187
Malibu, CA 90265

Wild West: M$, 50% freelance, pays on acceptance. Seeks nonfiction, columns/departments, photos/artwork. Subjects: history, humor, travel.

Web site: http://www.thehistorynet.com

Cowles History Group
741 Miller Drive SE, Suite D-2
Leesburg, Virginia 20175
email:cheryls@cowles.com

Working Mother Magazine: L$, 90% freelance, pays on acceptance. Seeks nonfiction. Subjects: Service, humor, child development, material pertinent to the working mother's predicament.

Home: http://www.workingmother.com

Guidelines:
http://www.workingmother.com/corp/writers_guide.shtml

Editorial Department:

Working Mother Magazine
260 Madison Avenue, 3rd Floor
New York, NY 10016

Yankee: L$, 60% freelance, pays on acceptance. Seeks nonfiction, fiction, columns/departments, photos/artwork. Subjects: New England, poetry, essays, gen interest, historical, humor, interview/profile, personal experience.

Home: http://www.yankeemagazine.com

Guidelines:
http://www.yankeemagazine.com/service/index.php

Yankee Magazine
Editorial Submissions
1121 Main Street
P. O. Box 520
Dublin, NH 03444

ZYZZYVA: S$, 100% freelance, pays on acceptance. Seeks only West Coast writers [author's note: hmmph.] for non-fiction, fiction, poetry.

Web site: http://www.zyzzyva.org

Guidelines: http://www.zyzzyva.org/zy-subs.htm

P.O. Box 590069
San Francisco, CA 94159-0069

Greeting Cards

Amberley Greeting Card Company: L$, 90% freelance, pays on acceptance. Needs: "Original, easy to understand, belly-laugh or outrageous humor. We sell to the 'masses."

Web site: http://www.amberleygreeting.com

Send for guidelines.

11510 Goldcoast Dr.
Cincinnati, OH 45249-1695

John Barlow, Publisher: M$, 50% freelance, pays on acceptance. Needs: "We want clean humor, nostalgic messages, loving, or sweet sentiments, and for Christmas and Easter cards, traditional captions [for supplied photos].

No Web site.

Send for guidelines.

2147 Windmill View Rd.
El Cajon, CA 92020

Cardmakers: S$, 100% freelance, pays on acceptance. Needs: "We like upbeat humor, skip sick or raunchy. Our customers use our cards to greet their customers. So a positive approach/result is desirable."

Web site: http://www.cardmakers.com

Send for guidelines.

P.O. Box 236
66 High Bridge Rd.
Lyme, NH 03768

DCI Studios: S$, freelance, pays on acceptance. Needs: "We are looking for fresh, new, innovative humor. We divide our humor needs into general jokes and woman's humor."

No Web site.

Send for guidelines.

8010 State Line Rd.
Leawood, KS 66208

Ephemera, Inc.: M$, 95% freelance, pays on acceptance. Needs: "Make us laugh out loud. We want provocative, irreverent and outrageously funny slogans. Topics include women's issues, the President, job attitudes, current events, pop culture, advertising satire, religion, pets, coffee, booze, pot, drugs, sexual come-ons and put-downs, aging, slacker angst, gays and lesbians, etc."

Web site: http://www.ephemera-inc.com

Guidelines: http://www.ephemera-inc.com/home.htm

P.O. Box 490
Phoenix, OR 97535

Koehler Companies, Inc. L$, 65% freelance, pays on acceptance. Needs: "Verse that works best is: topics such as golf, fishing, pets, and other passions. Sisters, Mom, Family, words to inspire without getting preachy, verse that speaks to women. Also verse for men, usually humorous. See our website for examples of our work."

Web site: http://www.koehlercompanies.com

Send for guidelines:

8758 Woodcliff Rd.
Bloomington, MN 55438

Novo Card Publishers: S$, 80% freelance, pays on acceptance. Needs: "A broad range of all-purpose types of cards."

Web site: http://www.novocard.net

Guidelines: http://www.novocard.net/guide1.htm

3630 W. Pratt Ave.
Lincolnwood, IL 60712

Oatmeal Studios: M$, 85% freelance, pays on acceptance. Needs: "Will review concepts. Humorous material (clever and very funny) year-round."

No Web site.

Send for guidelines.

P.O. Box 138W3
Rochester, VT 05767

P.S. Greetings: S$, 100% freelance, pays on acceptance. Needs: humor.

Web site: http://www.psgreetings.com

Guidelines:
http://www.psgreetings.com/creative_guidelines.htm

5730 N. Tripp Ave.
Chicago, IL 60646

Renaissance Greeting Cards: M$, 25% freelance, pays on acceptance. Needs: "For humor, we avoid 'put down' type of jokes and try to stay positive. Target audience is women over 18 and Baby Boomers."

Now Web site.

Send for guidelines.

P.O. Box 845
Springvale, ME 04083

SNAFU Designs: L$, 80% freelance, pays on acceptance. Needs: "We use clever ideas that are simple and concisely delivered and are aimed at a sophisticated adult audience. Off-the-wall humor that pokes fun at the human condition. Please do not submit anything cute."

No website

Send for guidelines.

Box 16643
St. Paul, MN 55116

Suzy's Zoo: M$, 75% freelance, pays on acceptance. Needs: "Cards that make people smile, touches their heart no matter what the occasion. Suzy's Zoo greeting cards are purchased primarily by women to give to their family and friends. We are looking for fresh, happy, witty verse that reflects the culture of today's family."

Web site: http://www.suzyszoo.com

Send for guidelines.

9401 Waples St.
Suite 150
San Diego, CA 92121

Other notable writer Web sites

Writing for DOLLARS!

http://www.writingfordollars.com

Writing for DOLLARS! focuses on the business side of writing (making money). As much as we all want to write for the sheer joy of it, prestige and accolades do not put bread on the table. Read *Writing for DOLLARS!* to find current markets that pay; how to market what you write and earn more; tips for entering high paying markets; and interviews with successful writing professionals.

Sponsors quarterly writing contests for cash and book prizes. Also the home of *Chicken Writer* - http://www.awoc.com/chickenwriter.cfm

Sell Writing On-line

http://sellwritingonline.com

Discover how you can benefit from writing online with publishing opportunities that will keep you satisfied. New additions are added weekly.

University of Dayton Erma Bombeck Writer's Workshop

http://www.humorwriters.org

Freelance Writers

http://freelancewrite.about.com

The Write Market

http://www.writemarket.com

An online writer's market list - which has been online since 1996. Features regular writing news and six hundred listings for markets, literary services, agents and editors, writing terms, articles and publishers in one place

The Scriptorium

http://www.thescriptorium.net

A virtual room for writers. In each monthly issue you'll find articles, interviews, exercises, book reviews, and more to help you become the best writer you can be.

The Writer Gazette

http://www.writergazette.com

A writer's resource site that provides tips, techniques, resources, articles, job postings, and more to help induce, improve, and promote your writing career.

References

Comedy Writing for Television & Hollywood. Milt Josefsberg. Harper & Row Publishers. 1987.

Laughing Matters: A Celebration of American Humor. Gene Shalit, Editor. Ballantine Books. New York. 1987.

Non Campus Mentis. Professor Anders Henriksson. Workman Publishing. New York. 2001.

On Writing. Stephen King. Pocket Books. New York. 2000.

The Comic Mark Twain Reader. Charles Neider, Editor. Doubleday & Company. New York. 1977.

The Complete Guide to Writing & Selling Magazine Articles. Peggy Moss Fielding, Dan Case. AWOC.COM Publishing. Denton, Texas. 2001.

The Elements of Style. Third Edition. William Strunk Jr., E. B. White. MacMillan Publishing. New York. 1979.

Treasury of Atrocious Puns. Bennet Cerf. Harper & Row Publishers. New York. 1968.

About the Author

Phil Truman was born a poor white child in rural Oklahoma. Through perseverance, hard work, good fortune, and a fair amount of butt-kissing, he has risen to where he is today - a poor white man in urban Oklahoma.

As a freelance writer for over two decades, Phil has written humor columns and features for several newspapers, as well as regional and national magazines. He is best known as the "voice" of Chicken Writer, producing the gags for his and Chicken Writer's Co-Creator Dan Case's critically acclaimed writer's cartoon appearing everywhere on the Internet—published by AWOC.COM. Phil is the author of two novels, a collection of short stories, and creator of the award-winning weekly Internet humor column "ROFLing with Phil."

Phil, the father of two grown children, lives in Broken Arrow, Oklahoma with his patient and long-suffering wife of thirty years, Darlene.

More writing books from AWOC.COM

The Complete Guide to Writing & Selling Magazine Articles by Peggy Fielding and Dan Case – US $19.95 – The definitive guide for those who write for magazines. Over 300 markets are included.

Be Your Own Book Doctor by Robin Conley – US $9.95 – Learn to be your own book doctor so you can cure what ails your writing.

Confessing for Money by Peggy Fielding – US $14.95 – Writing and selling to the **SECRET** short story market.

Magic Steps to Writing Success by Charles W. Sasser – US $14.95 – Five magic steps toward becoming a successful writer-Discipline; Inspiration; Goals; Ideas; and Craft.

To purchase these titles, go online to AWOCBooks.com or send a check or money order for the purchase price plus US $4.00 for S & H (Canada US $5.50) to:

AWOC Books
P.O. Box 2819
Denton, TX 76202

Printed in the United States
59310LVS00002B/33

9 780970 750785